To Sudi & Tony,

For a wonderful weekend of friendship & wine.

Love,

Dana & Rich

The Champagne Cookbook

The Champagne Cookbook

ADD SOME SPARKLE
TO YOUR COOKING
AND YOUR LIFE

By Malcolm R. Hébert

PUBLISHED BY
THE WINE APPRECIATION GUILD

OTHER BOOKS PUBLISHED BY THE WINE APPRECIATION GUILD,
1377 Ninth Ave., San Francisco, CA 94122:

EPICUREAN RECIPES OF CALIFORNIA WINEMAKERS
GOURMET WINE COOKING THE EASY WAY
ADVENTURES IN WINE COOKERY
FAVORITE RECIPES OF CALIFORNIA WINEMAKERS
WINE COOKBOOK OF DINNER MENUS
EASY RECIPES OF CALIFORNIA WINEMAKERS
THE POCKET ENCYCLOPEDIA OF CALIFORNIA WINE
IN CELEBRATION OF WINE AND LIFE
WINE CELLAR RECORD BOOK

Managing Editor: Donna Bottrell
Contributing Editor: Ken Hoop
Illustrations: Susann Ortega
Design: Colonna, Caldewey & Farrell
Photography: Bill Miller

ISBN 0-932664-07-5

Library of Congress Catalog No.: 80-51653

First Printing: 1980

MANUFACTURED IN THE UNITED STATES OF AMERICA

Table of Contents

Foreword

The people who make Champagne are the nicest, most generous and considerate people I have ever had the pleasure of meeting. And their product is the nicest, most generous and considerate wine you can serve to your friends.

Both American and French Champagne producers have been kind enough to share their treasured recipes with me; many of the recipes are published here for the first time.

A special thanks to my wife Yvonne and our four children Mary Louise, Chris, Mark and James for helping me test and taste the recipes in this book. Their candor in tasting was greatly appreciated.

To Tom Kruse, who was kind enough to devise a special Champagne recipe especially for this cookbook adding his talents to the fun of Champagne.

And to Ken Hoop of the Wine Appreciation Guild, whose attention to detail, imagination and skill have helped this book become a reality.

Malcolm R. Hébert

Thomas Kruse
4390 Hecker Pass Road
Gilroy, California 95020

Dear Mal,

Enclosed is recipe for <u>Champagne Occidental</u>

Ingredients: 2 Bottles Thomas Kruse Champagne Natural (chilled)
1   can ripe pitted olives
6   slices stale bread
1   can whole kernal corn
5   eggs
1   can cranberry sauce
1   can chunk light tuna
1   pkg. onion soup mix
1/2 jar mustard
2/3 jar hot dog relish
1/2 pint very old garlic flavored dip.
1   telephone in working order

Directions: 1. Carefully open a bottle of champagne and pour two glasses (one for you and one for your friend or spouse) 2. Be sure to use clean hollow-stem tulip glasses or flutes — never, <u>never</u> use those dumb shallow little glasses that you always get at wedding receptions. 3. Propose a toast. 4. Sit down (you've had a long day). 5. Contemplate carefully the above ingredients <u>because</u> thats all you have in the house.
6. Have another glass of champagne. 7. Consider your options;
A. Put everything in a blender and see what happens, B. Go to the store for more food (its raining), C. Go on a fast, D. None of the above.
8. Pour another glass of Champagne and send out for Chinese Food reserving the second bottle for dinner.

Mal, I hope its not too late   Tom Kruse

I

Introduction

Cooking With Champagne

Champagne is a wine to make you remember the past, look to the future and live to enjoy today.

It is the "glamour girl" of the wine family. It is the wine for all occasions, birthdays, weddings, anniversaries, ship launchings, intimate suppers, midnight snacks, picnics, parties, afternoon tête-à-têtes; the list is endless.

Champagne has been called an incomparable wine, the wine of wines, the wine divine. It is delicate, distinctive and the darling of wine lovers throughout the world. It mixes and marries in the kitchen as well as on the table.

To make Champagne, the Champagnemaster assembles a cuvée, or a blend of still wines to match the style of the firm. He adds a mixture of sugar and yeast to the wines and bottles them. Now they begin the secondary fermentation. When the yeast and sugar have done their work, they fall as sediment and are worked down to the neck of the bottle. The neck is frozen in brine and the sediment is popped out of the bottle as a plug. A small amount of syrup called a "dosage" is added to the wine. The amount of syrup determines how dry or sweet a bottle of Champagne will become. Now the final cork and wire hood is placed on the bottle and the Champagne is given time to rest before it is shipped. This method of making Champagne is called *la methode champanoise*.

Science has played an important part in Champagne making. There is a German Champagne making process called Carstens transfer process. It starts out like la methode champanoise, but when the time comes for the sediment to be removed, the bottles are emptied into a holding tank. The wine is then filtered and returned to the bottles with a dosage.

A French method, called the Charmet process or bulk process, lets the wine undergo a secondary fermentation in huge glass lined tanks. It is then filtered and bottled.

Aside from the technical aspects of Champagne making, other factors play an important role. These include the sun, soil, rain, ageing process, blending of the wines, etc.

No two Champagnes are exactly alike and therefore preference for one Champagne over another is a matter of personal taste. Champagne varies from a light pale color to a deep gold; from very dry called "natural" to the very sweetest called "doux" or douce; from a little fruit to a great deal and from a little yeast to a lot of yeast.

The best way to find out what Champagne pleases your purse and palate, is to hold a Champagne tasting. Invite 10 friends and have each one bring a different bottle of Champagne. Use tulip shaped glasses, which show off the tiny bubbles, and pour a few ounces of Champagne into the glass. After tasting the Champagnes, you will be able to narrow the 10 down to two or three Champagnes. Refresh your mouth with some dry bread and taste the remaining, and you should be able to decide which Champagne you like best.

Cooking with Champagne poses no special problems for the chef. Use the Champagne you like best in the recipes. All the amounts are accurate to taste, but if you like a little more Champagne in the recipe, by all means use it. Everyone has different taste references. Much depends upon how you were reared at home, what you ate as a child, what your parents were fed, too. The recipes here are culinary guidelines to perfection. You will add the final touch.

II

Cocktails, Drinks and Punch

A glass or two of Champagne with breakfast is a splendid way to start any day.

The man who believes that is Richard H. Elwood, President, Llords & Elwood Winery. And it's a great idea. If you haven't tried it, you should. Sunday is a good day to start. Sleep late. When awake, pour yourself an ice cold glass of Champagne. Sip it slowly. Savor it! Relish the fact that you have indulged yourself in a Champagne taste treat. Remember, this is the way royalty will treat you, so you might as well get used to it.

Champagne for breakfast, Champagne for lunch, Champagne for dinner: what a great way to live.

More and more Americans are giving up hard liquor drinks before lunch and dinner in favor of wine. And Champagne is one of the most popular of all the pre-luncheon and dinner drinks.

Champagne is the perfect aperitif. Alone, it satisfies the palate as well as stimulates the appetite. Mixed with other ingredients, it becomes an enticing cocktail.

Punches are believed to have originated in India. There are many variations on the theme, but the largest punch ever made was by an English sea captain. He used 80 casks of brandy, 9 casks of water, 25,000 large limes, 80 pints of lemon juice, 1,300 pounds of sugar, 5 pounds of nutmeg and one large cask of Malaga wine.

To serve the 6,000 guests from such a vast marble basin, small boys used a rowboat floating on the vast alcoholic sea, but the fumes overcame them and they had to be replaced every 15 minutes.

The secret of making a good punch is to make each batch separately. If there is a little of the old punch in the bottom of the bowl, either drink it or throw it away. Don't let it stand in the bowl while you make a new batch, for it only dilutes the next batch.

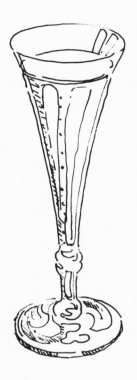

GOOD MORNING AMERICA

Francellene Baine Roper of Brookside Vineyard Company in Old Guasti, California, claims the best way to start any day is with her favorite recipe—Good Morning America.

Ice cubes
1 can frozen orange juice diluted
*   with 2 cans water*
1 fifth Guasti Extra Dry or Brut
*   Champagne*

Fill three large tumblers with ice cubes. Add half the orange juice and half the Champagne. Serves 3.

CHAMPAGNE COCKTAIL

If you want to surprise your friends, here is a new way to serve a simple Champagne Cocktail.

1 glass of chilled Champagne
1 wooden skewer alternately
*   lined with a black grape, white*
*   grape, black grape, etc.*

Place the skewered grapes in a chilled Champagne glass. Pour over grapes chilled Champagne. Serves 1.

GREYSTONE COCKTAIL

This punch is the most popular beverage among the Christian Brothers employees. It is served routinely at their social gatherings and is reported to be a "guaranteed social relaxant".

1 fifth bottle Christian Brothers
*   Brut Champagne*
1½ cups Christian Brothers
*   Brandy*
2 quarts Ginger Ale

Place a block of ice in punch bowl. Slowly add other ingredients. Add fresh strawberries for color and taste. A special punch for a very special occasion.

Chateau St. Jean is the newest California winery to produce Champagne. They have named Edgar "Pete" Downs, former research enologist at Korbel Champagne Cellars, to oversee the entire construction and production of their new sparkling wine operation.

The first St. Jean sparkling wine, vintage 1980, will not be released until 1983. However, while you are waiting, Mr. Downs suggests the following for a nice Sunday brunch or to be sipped with Eggs Benedict.

MIDMORNING DELIGHT

1. Put a fresh peeled freestone peach half in a sparkling wine glass.

2. Fill the glass with premium California sparkling wine and enjoy.

Thanks, Pete. We'll drink to that!

BRANDY CHAMPAGNE COCKTAIL

The late Earle MacAusland, Editor and Publisher of Gourmet Magazine helped Americans to lead a better life. He pioneered a magazine that turned Americans into gourmets. He taught them to appreciate fine wines, restaurants and recipes.

Not too many years ago, MacAusland published a Brandy Champagne cocktail recipe in one of his issues of Gourmet. It is one of the brightest beginnings you can offer a friend. Here is the original recipe, just as it was published in Gourmet Magazine.

Moisten the rim of a Champagne glass with lemon juice, invert it into a small dish of sugar and chill the glass. In the glass, combine 2 tablespoons of brandy and 2 teaspoons sugar syrup*. Fill the glass with chilled Champagne. Garnish with a twist of orange peel. Makes 1 drink.

* SUGAR SYRUP

1 cup water
1 cup sugar

Combine ingredients in a saucepan and cook until sugar is dissolved in the water. Let mixture cook over moderate heat for 5 minutes. Can be sealed in glass jars and kept indefinitely. Makes 2½ cups.

SPARKLING COLORS

New ways to serve Champagne cocktails or cocktails using Champagne are interesting. Valeria Furino, who is the international food consultant and food designer for Paul Masson has created a new Champagne based drink.

2 parts apple cider
5 parts Paul Masson Extra Dry
Champagne
1 long stick of cucumber
1 wedge of Red Delicious apple

Pour cider into Champagne glass. Top with Champagne and garnish with cucumber and apple. Serves 1.

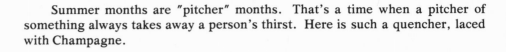

CHAMPAGNE QUENCHER

Summer months are "pitcher" months. That's a time when a pitcher of something always takes away a person's thirst. Here is such a quencher, laced with Champagne.

>   *1 fifth chilled Champagne*
>   *4 cups chilled orange juice*
>   *Ice cubes*

Combine all ingredients in a large pitcher. Makes 14— ½ cup servings.

FLAMINGO

Jim Lucas who is Vice President and Director of Communications for Fromm and Sichel, the world wide distributors of Christian Brothers of California wines and brandies has successfully demonstrated this new cocktail on television.

>   *1 canned peeled apricot, pitted*
>   *and diced*
>   *1 Tbsp. apricot syrup (from can)*
>   *2 Tbsp. crushed ice*
>   *2 oz. Christian Brothers Cham-*
>   *pagne Rose, chilled*

Place the first three ingredients in a blender and whirl until smooth. Pour into a wine glass and fill with Champagne. Serves 1.

CHILLING CHAMPAGNE

Chilling several bottles of Champagne for a large party can tax a refrigerator. So, a big supply of ice cubes or crushed ice can come in handy. In addition, ice cubes can chill a single bottle of Champagne in 30 minutes while the refrigerator takes up to two hours. Place the unchilled Champagne in a suitable tub or container. Spread around the bottle or bottles the ice cubes. Fill with cold water. In 30 minutes or less, the Champagne should be chilled.

GALAXIE COCKTAIL

If you are a fruit buff and like Champagne, here's a new combination that can be served either before or after dinner.

½ cup fresh pineapple
1 orange, peeled, seeded and
*   sliced*
½ cup fresh strawberries
3 Tbsp. sugar
¾ cup brandy
1 bottle Champagne, chilled

Chop the first three ingredients into a fine dice. Sprinkle with sugar. Add brandy, mix well and chill one hour. Divide the mixture evenly into six chilled Champagne glasses. Pour chilled Champagne into the glasses. Serves 6.

ANNIVERSARY COCKTAIL

Here's another before dinner cocktail that comes from Dick Elwood, President of Llords & Elwood Winery. This is especially good on warm sunny afternoons.

½ oz. grapefruit juice
½ oz. rum
½ oz. brandy
½ oz. Cointreau
Crushed ice
Llords & Elwood Champagne

Put the first four ingredients into a cocktail shaker along with some crushed ice. Shake well and strain into chilled Champagne glass. Fill with Llords & Elwood Champagne. Serves 1.

Dom Perignon, a Benedictine monk, has often been credited with having invented Champagne. What is little known, is that he was the first to blend the produce of different vineyards in the Champagne region so as to obtain a stock whose quality would be superior to any of the individual elements from which it was composed. This practice is still being used in both France and California and other parts of the world.

ROYAL PUNCH

Here are two punches from the kitchens of The Taylor Wine Company.

1 block of ice
2 bottles Taylor New York State
Sauterne, chilled
1 cup Brandy
1 bottle Taylor New York State
Extra Dry Champagne

Put the block of ice into a punch bowl. Pour chilled wine and brandy over the block: stir to blend well. Pour Champagne into the bowl. Float a few fresh strawberries or mint leaves in the punch. Serve in punch cups. Makes 22 four ounce servings.

HOW BIG IS A CHAMPAGNE BOTTLE?

Split
(½ pt.) 6 ½ oz.

Half Bottle
(⅘ pt.) 13 oz.

BRIDAL PUNCH

3 cups cranberry juice, chilled
1 bottle Taylor New York Lake
Country White, chilled
1 bottle Taylor New York State
Pink Champagne, chilled

Pour cranberry juice and Lake Country White over ice mold into punch bowl. Carefully add Pink Champagne. Garnish with fresh strawberries. Makes 20 four ounce servings.

CREOLE CHAMPAGNE PUNCH

The Creoles and Acadians (Cajuns) take their food and drink seriously. These folks have blended their talents into what has been called "Louisiana French style" cooking. It is spicy, well prepared, and some of the best food in the United States. They also care about what they drink and in the cool after-

Full Bottle
(⅘ qt.) 26 oz.

Magnum
(2 bottles) 52 oz.

noons, when the hot Louisiana sun is ready to set, there is nothing so refreshing in the garden as a glass of special Creole Champagne Punch.

> *1 fresh pineapple, peeled*
> *1 pint fresh strawberries, washed*
> *   and hulled*
> *1 Lb. super fine sugar*
> *1 cup strained lemon juice*
> *1 cup strained orange juice*
> *½ cup Curacao*
> *1 fifth Champagne, chilled*
> *1 fifth dry white wine, chilled*
> *6 cups club soda*
> *Mint leaves*

Halve the pineapple. Cut one half into one inch wedges. Grate the other half. In a large punch bowl add sugar, lemon and orange juice, Curacao, and stir until sugar is dissolved. Add strawberries, Champagne, wine and remaining ingredients. Makes 5 quarts. NOTE: Ice can be added a little at a time so as not to dissolve the mixture.

Jeroboam
(4 bottles) 104 oz.

Tappit-Hen
(5 bottles) 128 oz.

WIDMER CHAMPAGNE PUNCH

Widmer's Wine Cellars in Naples, New York, sent along one of their favorite punch recipes which can be used for large receptions or weddings.

> *½ cup sugar*
> *1 cup water*
> *1-6 oz. can frozen lemon juice*
> *3-6 oz. cans frozen orange juice*
> *2 bottles Widmer Extra Dry*
> *   Mousse Sec Champagne*
> *1 qt. ginger ale*
> *1 qt. sparkling water*
> *1-4 oz. bottle maraschino*
> *   cherries & juice*
> *1 orange, sliced thin*
> *1 qt. lemon or orange sherbet*
> *Block of ice*

Heat water until sugar dissolves; cool. Combine fruit juices, Champagne, ginger ale, sparkling water, cherries and orange slices. Pour over block of ice. Drop sherbet by the spoonfuls into the punch or use a small ice cream dipper. Serves 50-60 people.

Rehoboam
(6 bottles) 156 oz.

Thank You Korbel

19

MINT SHRUB

Mint juleps are a popular drink in the Southern part of the United States. In fact, Louisville, Kentucky is actually the home of the julep. However, Almaden Vineyards has come up with an interesting version of the julep, using, naturally, Champagne.

½ cup mint leaves, crushed
2 Tbsp. sugar
4 oz. Apricot liqueur
8 oz. Almaden brandy
Ice
4 bottles Almaden Brut Champagne

Crush the mint leaves with the sugar. Add liqueur and brandy and let infuse for one hour. Put the ice in a punch bowl, add the mixture, and pour over it the Champagne. Serves 12 - 15 persons.

HOME MADE PUNCH

4-10 oz. packages of cherries
2 cups of brandy
Block of ice
4 bottles of your favorite rosé wine, chilled
2 bottles of Champagne, chilled

Thaw cherries, combine with brandy and chill 4 hours. Put ice in punch bowl and pour over it the brandy mixture, then add the rosé and Champagne. Serves 50.

HOW TO OPEN A BOTTLE OF CHAMPAGNE

Avoid shaking the bottle.

Remove the capsule covering the cork. Hold the bottle at a 45 degree angle making sure it is pointed away from you and other individuals. Place your thumb on top of the cap covering the cork. Loosen the wire hood by twisting the loop counter-clockwise. Lift thumb, remove hood, and place your thumb back on the cork. Place napkin or bar towel over hand and cork.

To open the Champagne, grasp the cork by the handle or knobby top. Now TWIST THE BOTTLE NOT THE CORK and let the cork come out with a "sigh" not a loud "pop". Continue to hold the bottle at the 45 degree angle for a moment. Now pour the Champagne into a glass. Fill the glass only ⅓ full.

Enjoy.

STRAWBERRY CHAMPAGNE PUNCH

Here are three quick and easy punches that you can prepare without having to do a great deal of advanced preparation.

1 small box strawberries
½ cup sugar
½ cup brandy
Juice of 1 lemon or lime
2 bottles of white wine
1 bottle Champagne

Wash and hull strawberries. Place in a large punch bowl. Add sugar, brandy, lemon/lime juice and one bottle of white wine. Chill 4 hours. Just before serving, add remaining ingredients. Place an ice cube in each punch cup and fill with punch. Serves 20.

THINK PINK

Pink Champagne, sometimes called Rosé Champagne, has been known as a party wine, a naughty wine and a lover's wine. You can take your choice.

Such Champagnes have been traced back, according to the British wine writer, Cyril Ray, to the late Victorian and Edwardian eras, describing their consumption as a "tradition already getting on for a century old."

How pink Champagne was created is a subject for debate. We like the idea of one old Champagne maker who said that the most suitable occasion to serve pink Champagne is in the evening when you are dining at a table decorated with a pink table cloth, pink flowers and pink candles and the menu includes lobster and strawberries.

PETER'S PUNCH

1-6 oz. can frozen lemonade
*   concentrate*
2 Tbsp. sugar
¼ cup Grand Marnier
1 bottle Champagne, chilled

Thaw concentrate and mix according to directions on the package. Place in large punch bowl. Add remaining ingredients. Place an ice cube in each punch cup and fill with punch. Serves 10.

PUNCH DE GALLE

Here are two punches that serve 40 people, and are very easy to make. In fact, if you have a large punch bowl you keep hidden throughout the year and only use for special parties, plan a party now. Both of these recipes use brandy and liqueurs.

3 bottles of Champagne
1 bottle club soda
6 ounces brandy
4 ounces Chartreuse
4 ounces Cointreau
Sugar to taste

Combine all ingredients. Mix well. Put a block of ice into the punch bowl and pour the punch over the ice. Serves 40 people.

CHARLEY'S CHARGE

This next punch is for men with stout and staunch stomachs. The recipe calls for four bottles of Champagne and two bottles of brandy. But, remember, it does serve 40 people.

8 Tbsp. sugar
Grated rind of 3 lemons
Grated rind of 1 lime
2 cups orange juice
½ cup lemon juice
2 bottles of Armagnac
2 cups Cointreau
4 bottles Champagne

Combine the first six ingredients in a bowl and let marry for one hour. When ready to serve, add Cointreau and Champagne and pour over a block of ice. Serves 40.

Champagne is the only wine to have a song expressly written for it. It is called "Champagne Charley" and entitled "The great comic song written and sung by George Leybourne" with the music by Alfred Lee.

The chorus goes:

Champagne Charley is my name
Champagne Charley is my name
Good for any game at night, my boys
Good for any game at night, my boys
Champagne Charlie is my name
Champagne Charlie is my name
Good for any game at night, boys:
  who'll come a join me in a spree.

Circa 1901

GERMAN COLD DUCK

Did you know that Cold Duck is a German Punch that relies on the spritz, or tingling quality of German Moselle wines? Its name comes from the appearance of the punch bowl which was decorated with a spiraling lemon peel arranged to resemble the head and body of a duck.

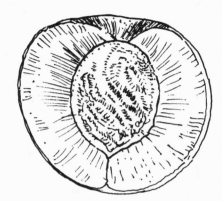

> *2 Tbsp. lemon juice*
> *4 Tbsp. sugar*
> *1 large lemon*
> *2 bottles Moselle wine, chilled*
> *1 bottle dry Champagne, chilled*

In a large punch bowl combine the lemon juice and sugar until the sugar is dissolved. To make the "duck", cut the rind partially off the lemon in a long spiral neck, starting with one slice about 1 inch down from the top to form a cap or head. Place the cap over the side of the punch bowl and the whole lemon in the bottom. Pour the chilled Moselle and Champagne into the punch bowl, stir. Place an ice cube in each punch cup and pour in punch. Serves 24.

MRS. KOLAROVICH'S PEACH BOWL

Jelena Kolarovich, wife of George Kolarovich, the winemaster for Perelli-Minetti Winery in Delano, California, says that in Balkan cooking, club soda is often used to add a lightness to dishes. But, for the past 20 years she has substituted Champagne for soda, claiming it makes an elegant difference. How true!

> *6 very ripe peaches, peeled and*
> *sliced into eighths*
> *¼ cup sugar*
> *½ cup brandy*
> *3 bottles of Champagne, chilled*

Put sliced peaches in punch bowl. Sprinkle with sugar and brandy. Let stand for several hours. Pour in chilled Champagne. Serve with a slice of peach in each glass. Makes 30 servings.

Champagne is so glamorous that WINE: An Introduction for Americans, waxes quite poetic about it:

"The bottles of finished wine are generally stored horizontally for a brief period to set the cork into the familiar mushroom shape and allow detection of leakers. Further aging at this stage appears to have no great advantage. The bottle is now dressed in its label, foils and furbelows and sent off to grace elegant occasions, launch ships and brides, and otherwise make all this trouble worthwhile. Since an estimated 120 hand operations go into each bottle of fermented-in-the-bottle Champagne and its production requires skill and involves an appreciable risk of loss, it will always be a costly product..." More Fun With Wine, 1973.

Costly, perhaps.....Enjoyable, unquestionably.

LUCHOW'S MAY WINE BOWL

Luchow's restaurant in New York is one of the great German food houses. Every spring, the restaurant features its special May Wine Bowl, a punch flavored with the magic herb, woodruff. This special herb is usually found in the spring at specialty markets. A good substitute is a small piece of cinnamon stick, or a tablespoon of cloves.

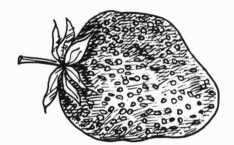

> *½ cup dried woodruff*
> *¼ cup superfine granulated*
>   *sugar*
> *½ cup brandy*
> *2 bottles Rhine wine*
> *1 bottle Champagne*
> *½ cup whole, fresh strawberries*
> *Ice cubes*

Tie the woodruff in a small piece of cheesecloth. Put it in a large bowl and add sugar, brandy and 1 bottle of the Rhine wine. Cover and let stand overnight. Next day strain mixture into a large punch bowl. All remaining ingredients, stir. Makes 20-½ cup servings.

WEIBEL'S WEDDING PUNCH

Fernand Point was one of the world's greatest chefs. The Restaurant de la Pyramide was an extraordinary place to dine and today still holds its 3 ★ ★ ★ from the Michelin Guide. The hour before lunch was the hour M. Point liked best. He wore a large black bow tie, and on the table was a magnum of Champagne in a silver bucket. It was here that Champagne, companionship and good talk were welcome. Here he would sit with a guest and discuss "la grande cuisine". And during that time he would compose a menu for you, which always included Champagne.

Fred Weibel, whose Weibel Champagne Vineyards makes hundreds of thousands of bottles of Champagne under his own label as well as many other labels, has some special punches he and his family serve to guests. The amount of punch you will need depends upon the number of guests and the length of time the punch will be served. On the average, you may assume a guest will consume approximately three 3 oz. servings during a one hour period.

Here's Fred's wedding punch.

> *3 bottles of Weibel Champagne*
> *1 bottle Weibel Sauterne*
> *2 bottles sparkling water*

Mix well over a block of ice. Makes 45 - 3 oz. servings.

CHAMPAGNE BRUNCH PUNCH

The Christian Brothers of California have devised a single beverage that can be drunk throughout a brunch party.

2 lemons
2 oranges
1 (1 lb. 4 oz.) can pitted dark
*   sweet cherries*
1 pint Christian Brothers brandy
1 bottle Christian Brothers Rhine
*   wine*
1 bottle Christian Brothers Brut
*   Champagne, chilled*
Strawberries for garnish

Cut peel from 1 lemon and 1 orange in long spirals. Squeeze juice from fruits to make ⅓ cup lemon juice and ¾ cup orange juice. Combine juices and spirals of peel, undrained cherries, brandy and Rhine wine in a bowl, cover and refrigerate overnight. When ready to serve guests, pour mixture over a chunk of ice in a large brandy snifter or punch bowl. Add Champagne and strawberries. Makes 24 (3¾ oz.) servings.

ROMAN PUNCH

One of the world's great gourmets was Grimod de La Reyniere. He expressed his belief that the purpose of a spiritous drink taken between courses was to brace "the fibres of the stomach and to accelerate the peristaltic movement which produces digestion". By 1860, the upper English class had adopted this custom at their formal dinners. This was one of their favorites.

1 quart lemon ice
8 Tbsp. Pernod
2 bottles of Champagne

Put ½ cup of the lemon ice in each of 8 tall glasses. Pour over 1 Tablespoon of the Pernod. Slowly pour the Champagne into each glass. Stir with a long handled spoon. Serves 8.

QUIZ?
What wine was sometimes called "vin diable" or devil wine, just because it exploded in the Spring?
You peeked!
Champagne, of course.

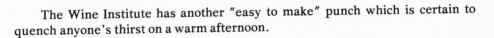

WINE INSTITUTE PUNCH

The Wine Institute has another "easy to make" punch which is certain to quench anyone's thirst on a warm afternoon.

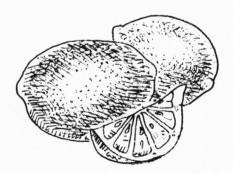

2 cups sliced fresh/frozen peaches
2 cups melon balls
2 cups halved fresh strawberries
¼ cup sugar
1 Tbsp. lemon juice
2 bottles California Chablis, chilled
2 bottles California Champagne, chilled

Combine fruits, sugar and lemon juice. Add Chablis and chill 4 hours. Put mixture into a punch bowl and add Champagne. Serves 30 (4 oz. servings).

A FAVORITE PUNCH

Here's a strawberry punch that you can whip up in just about as much time as it takes to write out the recipe.

1 qt. strawberries
½ cup sugar
½ cup Armagnac
Juice of 1 lemon
1 bottle of white wine
2 bottles of Champagne
Ice cubes

Wash and hull strawberries. Place them in a punch bowl. Top with sugar, Armagnac, lemon juice and the white wine. Chill 3 hours and then add remaining ingredients. Serves 15 people.

Hors d'Oeuvres

Caviar has always been considered the greatest accompaniment to Champagne. They are a combination so famous that there is a club in Chicago called the Champagne and Caviar Club. They meet only once a year and on that day feast on pounds of fresh Beluga Caviar washed down with bottles of French and California Champagne.

Caviar isn't the only first course that marries well with Champagne. Versatility is Champagne's second name for it lends itself to almost all first courses. Some courses do not help Champagne show its better side such as Indian curries, Spanish or Mexican hot sauces, and the spicy hot Szechuan cooking.

Even in the most modest of French families, hors·d'oeuvre may consist of the odds and ends of yesterday's meat, fish and vegetables. They are flavorfully sauced, spiced and served attractively in small dishes or even sectional trays. They are designed to pique the appetite and not satiate it.

My family loves a pork roast. I always buy a pork roast that will serve more than my family will eat. The reserve pork roast is made into a paté, along with some onion, garlic, mayonnaise, salt, pepper, sour cream and Champagne. It is allowed to marry for at least a day before it is served. You can do the same with chicken, steak, veal or vegetables.

The bible of cooking, Larousse Gastronomique list some 34 pages of hors d'oeuvres that you can make. This unique book claims that if you are having a heavy dinner or lunch, only light hors d'ouevres should be served. However, it is possible to serve a variety of hors d'ouevres along with Champagne to make a perfect lunch.

Champagne does lend itself admirably to those recipes that call for the addition of Champagne.

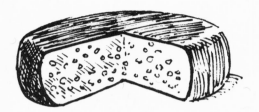

CHAMPAGNE PRUNES

36 prunes
36 pieces of Swiss cheese, 1 inch
  long and ½ inch thick
36 pieces of bacon, each piece
  5 inches long
½ bottle of Champagne
Toothpicks

In a medium sized sauce pan, soak the prunes in Champagne for two hours. Cover, bring to the boil, cool and remove prune pits. Reserve the liquid. Fill each prune with a single piece of cheese. Wrap each prune with a single slice of bacon. Skewer the prunes to hold the bacon. Broil the bacon wrapped prunes over charcoal or under the oven broiler. While the prunes are broiling, reduce the reserved liquid by half. When the prunes are done, serve with reduced sauce. Serves 6.

"Champagne is the only wine a woman can drink and still remain beautiful."
Madame Pompadour, 1755

CHAMPAGNE SAUSAGES

There's an old recipe that uses baby pork sausages with chicken called Poulet Pompadour. It was named in honor of Madame Pompadour because of her fondness for chicken and little pork sausages. We have eliminated the chicken and added Champagne.

18 baby pork sausages
½ bottle of Champagne

In a small sauce pan cook the sausages in Champagne for 8 minutes. Drain and reserve the liquid. Skewer the sausages and quickly brown them over charcoal or under the oven broiler. Baste with reserved liquid while cooking. When sausages are crisp, serve. Serves 6.

BLUE CHAMPAGNE DIP

Raw vegetables are very popular these days and people are always looking for special dips. Here's the new twist on an old theme.

¼ lb. blue cheese
1 cup sour cream
2 Tbsp. grated onion
¼ cup Champagne
1 Tbsp. lemon juice
Salt & White pepper to taste

Mash all ingredients together until they become a smooth paste. Pack in individual crocks or one large crock and chill 4 hours in the refrigerator. Serves 6. Special Note: Since blue cheeses are of different consistencies, you may have to use more sour cream or Champagne. The final result should be a dip that is easy to use.

CHAMPAGNEWURST

Liverwurst and Champagne? Yes, they make an excellent first course. You can pack them in individual crocks or one large crock. Serve with baby pickles, rye bread and butter.

1 lb. liverwurst
¼ cup Champagne (Approx.)
1 medium onion, grated
1 Tbsp. Dijon style mustard
½ tsp. minced dill pickle
Salt & Black pepper to taste

Thin liverwurst with Champagne. Add remaining ingredients, mix well and chill 3 hours in the refrigerator. Serves 6.

SHRIMPS PROVENCE

Shrimps swim in water, but we prefer them swimming in Champagne. Our first recipe allows the shrimp to marinate 24 hours before we serve them and the second recipe can be used as a first course or double as a fish course.

¾ cup olive oil
½ cup minced onion
2 cloves of garlic, minced
2 lbs. raw, washed, shelled, and
    deveined shrimp
Salt & Pepper to your taste
½ cup Champagne
¼ teaspoon dry mustard

In a medium sized sauce pan, heat the oil until hot. Add onions and garlic and sauté for 5 minutes. Add shrimp, salt and pepper and cook another 5 minutes. Allow mixture to cool for 20 minutes. Pour into a large bowl, add remaining ingredients. Stir well and let marinate in the refrigerator for 24 hours. Serves 6.

SHRIMPS ST. PIERRE

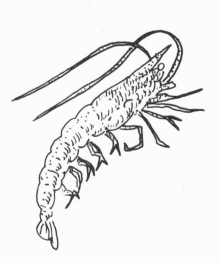

¼ lb. butter
1 cup onions, chopped
½ cup carrots, grated
1 Tablespoon parsley, minced
⅛ teaspoon thyme
Bay leaf
2 lbs. raw, washed, shelled and
    deveined shrimp
Salt & Pepper to your taste
¼ cup Brandy
1½ cups Champagne
1 Tablespoon tomato paste

In a large sauce pan, melt half the butter and sauté onions, carrots and parsley for 10 minutes. Add thyme, bay leaf, shrimp and salt and pepper, and cook for 5 minutes until the shrimp are done. Pour warmed brandy over the shrimp, ignite, and when the fire dies out, remove the shrimp with a slotted spoon. Keep shrimp warm. Add Champagne and tomato paste and cook for 5 minutes. Strain sauce. Return sauce and shrimp to saucepan and cook another 3 minutes over high heat. Add remaining butter, stir well. Serves 6.

OMELET AU CHAMPAGNE AVEC TROIS MOUTARDES

Ever taste a Champagne omelet? If you haven't, you're in for a real taste treat. This recipe suggests you roll the omelet and cut it into half inch rolls. You could serve the omelet in pie cut pieces, one inch pieces, or long strips. But serve it, you must.

4 eggs
1 teaspoon salt
3 grinds of fresh white pepper
2 Tablespoons Champagne
2 Tablespoons butter
3 mustards of your choice
Toothpicks

Beat the first four ingredients in a deep bowl. Heat the butter in a sauce pan and pour in the egg mixture. Cook on low heat until one side is done and then turn the omelet over and cook until the other side is done. Put the cooked omelet on a warm platter. Roll it up as tight as possible and cut it into half inch rolls. Skewer each roll with a toothpick. Serve with the three mustards. Serves 6.

PATÉ CHAMPAGNE

No cookbook would be complete without one good recipe for a French-like paté. This is a favorite of young and old alike.

½ lb. pork
½ lb. veal
½ lb. ham
4 slices of bacon
1 clove garlic, minced
½ cup Champagne
1 whole egg
Salt & White pepper to your taste
⅛ teaspoon basil
⅛ teaspoon oregano

Grind very fine the first four ingredients. Add remaining ingredients and whisk into a smooth paste. Put the mixture into a six inch loaf pan, packing it down tightly. Bake one hour in a 325° oven. Chill and unmold. Serves 6. SPECIAL NOTE: Sometimes, because of the food animals eat, pork, veal and ham may vary in water content. Unless you know your butcher, it is best to add the Champagne last. This way you will get the right mixture.

A NOTE ABOUT PATÉS

While patés may be considered a glamour girl in haute cuisine, there are a few things you should know about them.

First, the texture of the paté will depend upon water content of the meat you use. If the animal was fed a great deal of water prior to being butchered, some of the water may drip off into the paté.

Second, be as accurate as possible about measuring liquid when making a paté. It is better to have less liquid rather than finding your paté floating in liquid.

Third, the best ratio for meat to fat is one part fat and three parts meat. There are variations, but most chefs feel this is classically the best.

Fourth, blenders and food processors will give you the finest of patés, while using the old fashioned chef's knife will give you a rougher paté, called a country paté or woodsmen's paté.

Fifth, all patés improve with ageing. About one week in the refrigerator is all it takes for the flavors to marry.

Sixth, the density of the paté (especially a country paté) can be controlled by weighting it while it is chilling. A piece of wood cut to the inside measurements of the mold, wrapped with foil, and weighted with a household iron, a book, or some such item will do the trick.

FIGS WITH STARS

½ bottle Champagne
18 ripe figs
18 slices of bacon, each 5 inches
  long
Fresh ground pepper
Toothpicks

Marinate the figs in the Champagne for ½ hour. Broil the bacon until done, but not crisp enough so that it will break. Wrap the figs in the bacon slices and skewer with toothpicks. Grind pepper over the figs and serve. Serves 6.

NO TRUMP SPREAD

Millions of Americans play bridge. And about just as many have a "thing" about special dips for friends. Here's a quick and easy dip, complete with some Champagne.

1 cup sour cream
½ cup Champagne
1 Tablespoon chili sauce
1 small onion, grated
1 teaspoon chives, minced
1 tsp. Worcestershire
  sauce

Mix all ingredients together and chill in the refrigerator for 2 hours. Serves 6.

CHAMPAGNE OLIVES

1-15 oz. jar of green olives
Champagne

Drain the liquid from the olive jar and replace it with Champagne. Age the olives in the refrigerator for several days.

CELERY CHAMPAGNE

Now that celery can be had on a year around basis, it is frequently served as a first course. We stuff it with Champagne and Cheese.

2 large bunches of celery
¼ lb. butter
¼ lb. Roquefort or Stilton cheese
Black pepper to your taste
4 Tablespoons Champagne

Clean the celery and cut stalks into two inch pieces. Cream butter, cheese, pepper and Champagne. When well mixed, stuff cut celery stalks. Chill in refrigerator for 2 hours. Serves 6.

CHAMPAGNE AVOCADO SPREAD

If you really want to impress your friends, how about serving them a Champagne Avocado spread on Champagne toast, along with a glass of cold Champagne.

1 ripe avocado
½ lb. cream cheese
1 clove garlic, minced
1 Tablespoon lemon juice
2 Tablespoons Champagne
Salt & White pepper to your taste

Remove the skin and seed from the avocado. Mash the avocado meat with the remaining ingredients until a smooth paste is achieved. Spread this on Champagne Toast. (See below.)

CHAMPAGNE TOAST

1 loaf French bread
¼ lb. butter, melted
¼ cup Champagne
Pinch of dried basil

Cut the bread in half the long way. Mix melted butter with Champagne and basil and liberally coat the cut sides of the bread. Put the bread, cut side up, under the broiler and toast until brown. Cut pieces in 3 inch sizes and spread with Champagne Avocado spread. Serves 6.

HOW MUCH CHAMPAGNE

The best guide for serving Champagne is to allow ½ bottle per person for the minimum refreshment during an evening. This same amount is also adequate for a dinner party. For a New Year's Eve celebration, birthdays, or anniversaries, it is best to have a few extra bottles for emergencies.

If the unopened Champagne has been chilled in the refrigerator, it can be stored there for several weeks. To store opened Champagne, recork and use it the next day.

IV

Soups

Some two hundred years ago, soup was a very important food on the family table. It was the most sought after nourishment by farmers and woodsmen.

Today soups are re-appearing on menus once again. And no wonder, for they are an excellent way to begin a meal. They spark up one's appetite, prepare the palate for the next course and come in many styles: breakfast soup, dessert soup, wedding soup, Thanksgiving pumpkin soup and others.

Soup has played an important role in all cuisines of the world. Every cuisine has a soup in one form or another, whether it be made from water, stock, or vegetables.

There's an old country proverb which says:

A big man can carry a heavy load—

A good soup can carry a dinner

The word soup comes from the Latin *suppa*; the Dutch word is *sopen* and the German is *saufen*. Our word is derived from these three words for soup. In the broadest terms, they mean "to swallow."

No one actually knows when soups were begun. There is one story, maybe the greatest story about soups ever told. It goes like this:

Once upon a time a stranger came to town and in the middle of the square, set up a large kettle over a roaring fire. He filled the kettle with water and from his robe took a large nail and dropped it into the kettle. When asked what he was making, he replied, "I am making nail soup."

The townspeople gathered about him to watch. He tasted the water with the nail in it and said, "How much better this soup would taste if I had an old bone to put in the kettle." Someone in the crowd produced an old bone and the stranger dropped it into the kettle. He tasted the soup again and expressed the thought that a carrot would add a special flavor. An onlooker gave him a carrot.

He tasted the soup again and said aloud that perhaps a piece of meat, some celery, a small clove of garlic, and a cup of Champagne would enhance the flavor of the soup. All were offered for the pot.

When the soup was ready, the stranger let the townspeople taste the soup. They all nodded their heads saying, "Yes, you can make a very fine soup from a nail."

There was a time when people believed that a good soup could cure almost all a person's ills. Today, grandmothers all over the world are still prescribing soup as a restorative. We haven't changed that much.

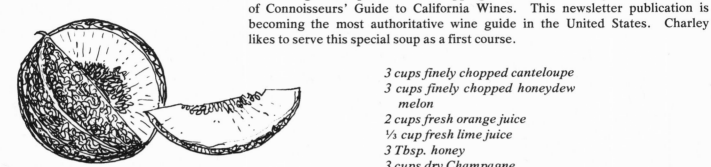

CHARLEY OLKEN'S SUMMER SOUP

One good soup for summer sipping comes from Charley Olken, co-editor of Connoisseurs' Guide to California Wines. This newsletter publication is becoming the most authoritative wine guide in the United States. Charley likes to serve this special soup as a first course.

3 cups finely chopped canteloupe
3 cups finely chopped honeydew
  melon
2 cups fresh orange juice
⅓ cup fresh lime juice
3 Tbsp. honey
3 cups dry Champagne
Whipped cream for garnish,
  slightly sweetened

Reserve 1½ cups each of canteloupe and honeydew. Put aside. Puree remaining 1½ cups each of canteloupe and honeydew with orange juice and lime juice. Chill. Just before serving, dilute the puree with the honey and Champagne. Then add reserved fruit. Serve with whipped cream. Serves 4 - 6 persons.

VINEYARD SOUP

This is a hearty soup and with French bread and Champagne, it is a meal in itself.

1 cup cooked rice
4 cups chicken stock, plus
  3 Tbsp. of stock
2 cups dry Champagne
2 egg yolks

Put the cooked rice in a 2 quart pan. Add chicken stock and Champagne. Slowly bring to the boil. Add the remaining chicken stock to the yolks, beating well. Add to the soup mixture. Stir. Serves 6.

BUBBLE TROUBLE
Here's to Champagne
It will cure all your troubles
A dollar's worth of wine
And three for the bubbles
                    Wine Institute
P.S. Did you know that you are paying a tax on the "bubbles" in a bottle of Champagne? That's right. The Senators and Congressmen you voted for are charging you for the bubbles in a bottle of Champagne. Now, doesn't that tell you something.

MOUNTAIN CLIMBER'S SOUP

If you are the hearty outdoor type, this might just be the soup for you.

4 Tbsp. butter
3 cups onion, minced
3 cups beef stock
4 cups Champagne
4 Tbsp. ripe Camembert cheese
4 eggs
6 Tbsp. California Brandy

In a large saucepan melt the butter and saute the onions until soft and slightly golden. Add stock and simmer 20 minutes over low heat. Add Champagne. Reheat. Add cheese and stir until all the cheese is melted. Beat eggs with brandy and when well mixed add to soup mixture. Stir briskly until well mixed. Pour into heated soup bowls. Serves 6.

CHAMPAGNE ONION SOUP

Everybody has their own recipe for onion soup. No two recipes or restaurants agree on all the ingredients for this famed French restorative. If they did, the soup would be boring. Here's one that's not.

3 cups white onions, chopped
fine
4 Tbsp. butter
5 cups beef stock
2 cups Champagne
Salt & Pepper to your taste

In a large sauté pan, cook the onions in the butter until they are soft. Put the onions in a large pot, add the stock, Champagne and salt & pepper. Bring to the boil, lower the heat and simmer, covered, for 3 minutes. Serves 6.

SPARKLING CREAM SOUP

Jack McDonald, Vice President of the Canandaigua Wine Company in Canandaigua, New York, a winery that has been producing Champagne since 1870, sent us this recipe using Champagne in the final presentation. Here's McDonald's recipe.

1 can (10½ oz.) condensed green
* pea soup, or the same amount*
* of homemade pea soup*
½ cup consomme
Dash of mace
Pinch of tarragon
½ cup heavy cream, slightly
* beaten*
1 cup Hammondsport Brut
* Champagne*
Croutons

Combine the first four ingredients in the blazer pan of a chafing dish. Blend thoroughly over medium heat bringing the mixture to a gentle boil. Fold in cream, reheat without boiling. Ladle into heated soup bowls and top with two to three ounces of Champagne. Add croutons. Serves 4.

BETTER CHEDDAR SOUP

One of the most novel of all soups is cheese soup. English by birth, cheese soup was another one of those creative flurries by a chef in obvious desperation. One doesn't think of cheese as a soup, just in the soup. Nevertheless, here are three cheese soups that make excellent first courses.

4 Tbsp. butter
½ cup minced onion
½ cup finely grated carrots
2 cups chicken stock
1 cup Champagne
¼ tsp. dry mustard
2 Tbsp. cornstarch
1½ cups half and half
1½ cups grated Cheddar cheese
Salt & Pepper to your taste

Francis Saltus once wrote:
Delicious, effervescent, cold Champagne,
Imprisoned sunshine, glorious and bright,
How many virtues in thy charm unite;
Who from thy tempting witchery can abstain?

In a saucepan, melt the butter and sauté the onions and carrots for 10 minutes. Add stock, Champagne and mustard. Mix well over low heat for 20 minutes. Mix cornstarch with a little of the cream and blend into the soup. Cook over low heat for 5 minutes. Add remaining ingredients and cook until the cheese is thoroughly melted. Serves 4. NOTE: This soup can be made as thick or as thin as you like it. Just add more chicken stock or Champagne.

VIENNESE CHEESE SOUP

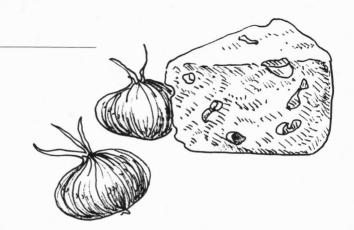

2 large onions
5 cups beef broth
1 cup Champagne
1 cup dry bread crumbs
2 cups grated Swiss cheese
1 Tbsp. flour
Salt & Pepper to your taste
¼ cup butter

Chop one onion fine. In a saucepan add the stock and Champagne and cook the chopped onion for 1 minute. Add bread crumbs, stirring all the time. Pour mixture into a blender and whip until smooth. Put mixture into a saucepan and heat until it simmers. Mix cheese with flour and drop cheese in small handfuls into the mixture. Stir until cheese is melted. Add remaining cheese, salt and pepper. Slice remaining onion into onion rings, sauté in butter until slightly golden. Pour soup into soup bowls and garnish with sautéed onion rings. Serves 6.

GRANDMOTHER'S OLD FASHIONED CHEESE SOUP

¼ cup butter
⅓ cup all purpose flour
4 cups whole milk
2 cups half & half
1 cup dry Champagne
2 cups grated Swiss cheese
2 cups grated Cheddar cheese
1 clove garlic, minced
1 Tbsp. salt
½ tsp. dry mustard
¼ tsp. fresh grated nutmeg
¼ tsp. fresh ground white
    pepper

**WHEN YOU COOK
WITH CHAMPAGNE.....**

* Never reduce Champagne by more than half. This way you avoid the wine becoming too tart. Example: Reduce 2 cups of Champagne called for in the recipe to only 1 cup.

* When adding Champagne to any dish, it will suddenly fizz. Pull the pan from the heat, wait ten seconds, and resume cooking.

* Champagne makes an excellent de-glazing agent for sautéed foods. The normal amount for de-glazing is about a half a cup.

* If you are not sure just what the dish will taste like after you have used Champagne, pour a little into a glass. Swirl the wine around until the bubbles have disappeared. Taste the wine. That's about what the final dish will taste like using Champagne.

* Always serve the same Champagne called for in the recipe.

* Use a Champagne in cooking that pleases your palate as well as your purse.

In a large saucepan, melt butter, stir in flour. When mixed, add milk and half & half. Cook over low heat for 8 to 10 minutes so the flour cooks. Add Champagne. Now add cheeses a cup at a time making sure they melt. After all the cheese has been added, put in remaining ingredients. Cook for another 5 minutes, making sure the mixture doesn't boil. Serves 6 to 8.

GOLD SEAL CHAMPAGNE ONION SOUP

6 oz. butter
3 lbs. onions, sliced thin
water
2 cloves garlic, chopped fine
4 cups chicken stock
½ bottle Gold Seal white
* Champagne*
Salt and Pepper to your taste
½ tsp. Accent
1 oz. Cognac
2 egg yolks
6 croutons
6 slices Swiss cheese

In a frying pan, melt half the butter and cook half the onion until they are brown, very soft and nearly candied. Add water from time to time to avoid burning. This may take 2 hours. Melt the balance of the butter in another frying pan, balance of onions, garlic and sauté until soft. Simmer for 1 hour. Pour into soup kettle and add broth, champagne and onions. Add salt, pepper, Accent, and cognac. Beat yolks until pale. Add 2-3 oz. of the soup to the yolks. Stir well. Keep soup hot. Add one crouton and one slice of cheese in each crock in which the soup has been poured. Grated Parmesan cheese can be used instead of the Swiss and the crocks can be put under a broiler until the cheese is melted. Serves 6.

CHAMPAGNE CONSOMMÉ

Simple soups that can be prepared quickly when company just happens to drop over are always welcome.

6 cups chicken stock
1 cup Champagne
Pinch of dried basil

In a saucepan bring all the ingredients to a gentle boil. Serve in individual heated soup bowls. Serves 6.

CHAMPAGNE BORSCH

At one time in European history, the Russians almost consumed as much Champagne as the French. The Russians have always loved Champagne and drink it like it was sparkling water. Today, Champagne consumption by the Russians is just behind their consumption of vodka.

2 (16 oz.) cans julienne beets
½ cup onion, minced
2 cups chicken stock
3 cups Champagne
2 tsp. salt
¼ cup lemon juice
3 Tbsp. sugar
Whipped cream

In a large saucepan combine the undrained beets, onions, stock, Champagne, salt, lemon juice and sugar. Bring to a quick boil and reduce to the simmer for 20 minutes. When cooked, chill for 5 hours. Serve cold in chilled soup bowls and top with a dollop of whipped cream. Serves 6.

CHAMPAGNE GAZPACHO

Gazpacho has been called the "national soft drink of Spain". And it might well be because of the enormous consumption of Gazpacho by the Spanish. There are some 50 versions of the famous soup, but somehow, Champagne slipped into this recipe; and maybe for the better.

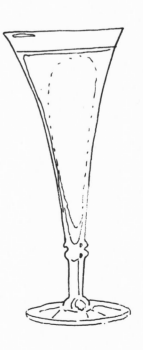

1½ lbs. peeled, seeded and
*   diced tomatoes*
½ cup onions, diced
2 cloves garlic, minced
1 cup green pepper, minced
¼ cup olive oil
¼ cup red wine vinegar
1 Tbsp. lemon juice
1½ cups Champagne
Salt & Pepper to your taste

In a blender purée first four ingredients. When mixed, pour into a non-metal bowl and add remaining ingredients. Mix well, and chill for 5 hours. Serves 6.

V

Fowl, Poultry

The Spanish said it best: "Chicken is the foundation of a good meal." Of course, no one would turn down quail, partridge, pheasant, squab or ruffled grouse as a substitute for chicken in any recipe.

Larousse Gastronomique, considered to be the bible of food, wine and cooking, has 22 pages devoted to cooking chicken with more than 260 recipes using the Asian originated bird. And, of course, the Wine Appreciation Guild series of Wine Cookbooks contains many pages of recipes cooking Poultry with wine.

Today, we eat more chicken than any other kind of fowl, simply because it is cheaper, easier to obtain, and lets our imagination soar.

Madame Pompadour did more to promote drinking and cooking with Champagne than anyone else in the world. She adored drinking it in vast quantities, and sometimes even took a bath in it.

Mistress to King Louis XV of France, Madame Pompadour loved anything cooked in Champagne. While she gorged herself on many dishes (it was not uncommon in that era to have five courses each composed of between 15 and 30 separate dishes), two were her favorite and only one was ever named after her (Poulet au Pompadour). The other favorite was Poulet en Champagne, chicken cooked in Champagne.

Why both of these recipes are seldom seen on restaurant menus is a mystery. They are easy to prepare and the use of an inexpensive non-vintage Champagne makes their cost to the customer reasonable.

No need to go to a restaurant. You can serve your family and friends these exceptional dishes tonight.

POULET AU POMPADOUR

*3 whole chicken breasts, skinned,
    boned and cut in half
12 small pork sausages
4 shallots or small white onions,
    minced
1½ cups dry Champagne
¾ cup chicken stock
3 egg yolks
¼ cup half & half
1 tsp. butter*

In a large saucepan put in the breasts, sausages, shallots, Champagne and stock. Bring to the boil, reduce to the simmer and cook covered for 15 minutes. Remove breasts and sausages to a warm platter and keep warm in a slack oven. Beat the yolks with the half & half. Stir a little of the hot liquid into the egg mixture beating constantly. Stir egg mixture into remaining hot liquid. Cook and stir for 3 minutes. Strain sauce. Add butter and mix well. Pour over chicken and serve. Serves 6.

CHICKEN MEDITERRANEAN STYLE

This dish is seasonal because it calls for tender mussels to be added 10 minutes before serving. When buying mussels, get them all the same size. You'll find they cook evenly and all open at the same time.

*¼ cup olive oil
1-3½ lb. chicken, cut up
4 cloves garlic, unpeeled
½ tsp. oregano
½ tsp. basil
1 cup dry Champagne
1 cup chicken stock
1 cup peeled, seeded tomatoes,
    chopped fine
2 lbs. medium sized mussels,
    trimmed of their beards
Salt & Pepper to your taste*

In a large saucepan, brown the chicken pieces in the oil. Add garlic, oregano, basil, Champagne, stock and tomatoes. Cover and cook for 30 minutes. Scrub the mussels making sure they are free from dirt and grit. Ten minutes before the chicken is done, add the mussels, salt and pepper, and cook the mussels until their shells have opened. Discard any mussels whose shells fail to open. Put the mixture onto a large platter. Serves 4.

CHAMPAGNE BASTING SAUCE

Outdoor barbecue fans, please note! Here is a great butter-Champagne basting sauce that will whet any appetite.

> *1 cup dry Champagne*
> *½ cup melted butter*
> *Salt & White Pepper to taste*

Blend everything together and baste chickens, squabs, quail, etc. every 10 minutes as they turn on the rotisserie. Makes enough for 1 chicken, three squabs, quail or other small birds. NOTE: You can add whatever herbs or spices you want to this mixture.

CANARD TOULOUSE

It's nice to know that duck breeders are giving us better and better ducks every year. And it's nice to know that ducks are becoming more and more popular at the dinner table. The Chinese and the French love duck and their recipes reflect that love. The Chinese don't use Champagne when they cook duck. The French do.

> *1-5lb. duck, left whole*
> *2 tsp. salt*
> *1 small orange, halved & peeled*
> *1½ cups dry Champagne*
> *½ cup sugar*
> *2 Tbsp. red wine vinegar*
> *¾ cup orange juice*
> *½ cup Grand Marnier*

Dry the duck with a paper towel. Rub salt on the outside of the duck and place the orange halves inside the duck's cavity. Put the duck on a shallow roasting pan and roast it at 425 degrees for 45 minutes turning the duck every 10 minutes. Pour off the fat and add the Champagne. Reduce heat to 325 degrees and roast 1½ hours, basting every 10 minutes. Combine sugar and wine vinegar and cook slowly in a saucepan until they become caramel colored. Add orange juice and Grand Marnier and cook another 5 minutes. Skim fat from pan juices and add to sauce. Remove and carve the duck. Serve sauce separately. Serves 4.

NORBERT MIRASSOU'S
CHAMPAGNE BASTES

SQUABS— Baste two squabs with one cup Mirrasou Brut Champagne. Continue to baste with the drippings until the desired degree of doneness is achieved.

TURKEYS— Pour a small amount of Mirrasou Brut Champagne in the bottom of the roasting pan and baste additional Champagne.

"The remaining Champagne is used to baste the chef," says Norbert.

CORNISH HENS IN CHAMPAGNE

Rock Cornish game hens burst into the culinary scene some 25 years ago, when a Connecticut breeder crossed a Plymouth Rock with a Cornish Game cock. The latter is a direct descendant of the famed Malayan game cock, considered to be the most ferocious of man's feathered friends.

Cornish hens are tender and are ready to eat just six weeks after birth. They weigh between a pound and 18 ounces. And, they lend themselves to a number of excellent recipes.

3 Rock Cornish game hens,
  cut in half
4 Tbsp. butter
3 Tbsp. Armagnac
Salt & Pepper to your taste
1 Tbsp. fresh tarragon (½ dried)
½ cup dry Champagne
½ cup whipping cream

Melt the butter in a large saucepan and brown the halved hens. Warm the Armagnac, pour over the hens and flame. When the flame dies down, add salt, pepper and tarragon. Cook over medium heat for 25-30 minutes. Remove the hens to a warm platter. Keep warm in a slack oven. Add Champagne, mix well and then add the cream. Cook on the simmer for 5 minutes. Strain sauce and pour over the hen halves. Serves 6.

CORNISH HENS VIEILLE MAISON

Here's another way to present hens to your friends. And it is simple to prepare and a delight to eat.

2 Cornish hens, halved
Salt & White pepper to your taste
6 Tbsp. butter
2 Tbsp. oil (salad, olive, walnut)
1½ oz. Armagnac
½ bottle Champagne
½ lb. fresh mushrooms, sliced
  thin
3 egg yolks
½ pint whipping cream

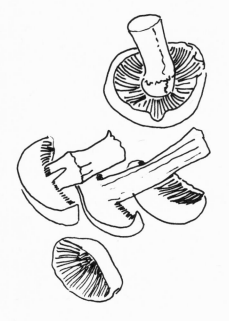

Salt and pepper the hen halves. In a Dutch oven or deep sauce pan melt 4 Tbsp. of the butter with the oil and sauté the hens until they are evenly brown. Heat Armagnac, ignite and pour over hens. After the flames die add the Champagne, and simmer for 30 minutes. Add mushrooms and cook another five minutes. Remove hens to a warm platter and keep warm in a slack oven. Add remaining 2 Tbsp. butter to the sauce to thicken it. Combine yolks and cream, mixing well, and stir into the sauce, but do not let it simmer or boil. Put the hens on a platter, garnish with baby carrots and cherry tomatoes. Serve the sauce separately. Serves 4.

CHOCOLATE HENS

Chocolate! Added to the sauce!

Yes, chocolate has been used in cooking for hundreds of years. In this case it adds a great flavor and taste to the final presentation. Don't let the name fool you.

⅓ cup olive oil
3 Rock Cornish game hens, cut
*   in half*
Salt & Pepper to your taste
12 small boiling onions
2 cloves garlic, minced
¼ cup Champagne
1 cup chicken stock
2 tsp. finely grated unsweetened
*   baking chocolate*

Heat the olive oil in a heavy casserole. Add salt & pepper and brown the hen halves all over. Transfer to a warm platter. Add onions and brown them all over. Remove the onions and add them to the hen halves. Drop in the casserole the minced garlic and cook one more minute. Add the hen halves, onions, Champagne and stock and cook about 25-30 minutes. Remove hen halves and onions to a warm platter and keep warm in a slack oven. Strain the sauce. Add the grated chocolate and cook for two minutes, stirring all the time. Pour sauce over hens. Serves 6.

CRÈME FRAICHE

Crème fraiche has suddenly become the darling of the jet set cooks. Some of the recipes in this book call for crème fraiche, because it adds to the flavor of the dish. It is also a better thickening agent than flour and has less calories.

There are many recipes for crème fraiche, but the best, in my opinion, comes from Michel Guerard, chef de cuisine at Eugenie-les-Bains, a Michelin 3★★★ restaurant and spa. This recipe first appeared in Guerard's book, *Cuisine Minceur*. It is the best of all I have tried.

MICHEL GUERARD'S CRÈME FRAICHE

1 cup sour cream
1 cup heavy whipping cream

Pour the sour cream into a wide mouth jar. Add the heavy cream and stir the mixture with a fork until well blended. Cover the jar and leave standing in the kitchen for 8 to 12 hours. Stir again and refrigerate for 12 hours or more. Makes 2 cups.

POULET AU CHAMPAGNE— 1

Here are two more versions of chicken in Champagne sauce. This time it is thickened with creme fraiche (see box) and an egg yolk.

> *1-4 lb. fryer cut up*
> *Flour*
> *4 Tbsp. butter*
> *¼ cup Armagnac*
> *Salt & Pepper to your taste*
> *½ cup chicken stock*
> *2 cups dry Champagne*
> *2 tsp. sugar*
> *2 Tbsp. crème fraiche*
> *1 egg yolk*

Flour the chicken pieces and sauté them in a saucepan until golden brown. Pour off fat. Heat Armagnac, pour over chicken pieces and flame. When flame dies, add salt, pepper, stock, Champagne and sugar. Cover and simmer 40 minutes. With a skimmer remove the chicken to a warm platter. Mix crème fraiche with egg yolk and add a little of the hot liquid to the mixture. Beat well. Add remaining liquid slowly until the sauce is medium in texture. Strain sauce through a fine sieve and pour over chicken. Serves 6.

POULET AU CHAMPAGNE— 2

Our second version uses tomato, basil and of course, Champagne.

> *1-4 lb. fryer cut up*
> *Salt & Pepper to your taste*
> *4 Tbsp. butter*
> *3 Tbsp. brandy*
> *¼ cup shallots or minced white onions*
> *1 cup Champagne*
> *1 large tomato, peeled, seeded and chopped fine*
> *½ tsp. basil*
> *1 egg yolk*
> *¼ cup heavy cream (whipping)*

Salt and pepper the chicken. Melt the butter in a large saucepan and sauté the chicken until brown all over. Heat the brandy, flame it and pour it over the chicken. Add shallots, Champagne, tomato and basil. Cover and cook at the simmer for 40 minutes. Beat the yolk with the cream in a bowl, pour off some of the liquid the chicken is cooking in, into the yolk mixture stirring to prevent curdling. You may use all the liquid, depending upon the thickness of the sauce you desire. Remove chicken to a warm platter, strain the sauce through a fine sieve and pour it over the chicken. Serves 6.

CHAMPAGNE STUFFING

If you like stuffing with your birds or chicken or other fowl, here is a special recipe that can be doubled, tripled, etc., depending upon the size of the fowl.

This recipe makes enough stuffing for a 2½-3 lb. chicken.

> *1 medium sized onion*
> *1 small clove of garlic*
> *1 shallot*
> *3 Tbsp. butter*
> *⅓ cup dry Champagne*
> *1 lb. pork sausage*
> *1 chicken liver*
> *Salt & Pepper to your taste*
> *1 Tbsp. minced parsley*
> *1 tsp. Quatre-Epices* (see next recipe)*

Sauté in the butter the onion, garlic and shallot until solft. Drain off butter. Cover the mixture with the Champagne and simmer until the liquid is reduced by half. Put the reduced mixture and the remaining ingredients into a food processor and mix well.

QUATRE-EPICES

This is one of the oldest French blends of spices. There are many versions but I always used the original recipe, as follows:

> *7 parts ground black pepper*
> *1 part fresh ground nutmeg*
> *1 part ground cinnamon*
> *1 part ground cloves*

Mix well and let marry for 2 weeks before using. Tightly sealed in a glass jar, this mixture will still be useful after one year.

"NEVER BEFORE,
HAVE SO FEW....."

The late Sir Winston Churchill preferred Pol Roger Champagne. He named one of his race horses "Odette Pol-Roger" in honor of Madame Pol Roger. When Sir Winston died, the Pol-Roger labels were black bordered.

CHICKEN VERONIQUE

Chicken breasts are considered to be the ultimate to serve one's guests. Indeed, the French call them "supremes", which is high praise for a barnyard bird. This next recipe uses chicken breasts, but halved Cornish hens, quail or partridge can be substituted.

> *2 Tbsp. salt*
> *½ tsp. white pepper*
> *3 Tbsp. flour*
> *3 whole chicken breasts, skinned,*
>   *boned and cut in half*
> *5 Tbsp. butter*
> *¾ cup dry Champagne*
> *¾ cup seedless white grapes*
> *3 Tbsp. blanched, sliced almonds*

Mix the salt, pepper and flour together and coat the breasts. Melt the butter in a large saucepan and quickly but lightly brown the breasts all over. Add Champagne, cover and cook 15 minutes. Add grapes and almonds and cook another five minutes. Serves 6.

EARL SINGER'S CHICKEN BREASTS IN CHAMPAGNE SAUCE

Chicken in Champagne sauce is one of those dishes that after you have made it, you have a desire to improvise, not because the dish is bad, but because you want variations on the theme.

Our first variation comes from Earl Singer, co-editor of Connoisseurs' Guide to California Wine. Earl sometimes serves this dish after a wine tasting.

> *3 whole chicken breasts, skinned,*
>   *boned and halved*
> *4 Tbsp. butter*
> *½ cup Champagne*
> *½ cup lemon juice*
> *½ cup heavy cream (whipping)*

Sauté the chicken breasts in the butter until done. Set breasts aside and keep warm. Add to the pan the Champagne and lemon juice. Reduce by half. Add heavy cream. Stir well. Strain and pour over breasts. Serves 6.

THE ALL CHAMPAGNE DINNER

If you are planning to have an all Champagne dinner, that is a five course repast with five different Champagnes, heed the following:

* Start with the driest of Champagnes and end with the sweetest.

* If you use a "Rosé" of Champagne or a "Blanc de Noir", make sure that you taste it before incorporating it into the menu. Some are bone dry and others slightly sweet.

* Remember that certain foods do not go with Champagne. Better try before you serve.

CHICKEN IN GOLD SEAL CHAMPAGNE

Charles Fournier is one of the pioneers of Champagne and is now Honorary President of The Gold Seal Wine Company.

1-3 to 4 lb. chicken
3 slices lean bacon, diced
¾ cup butter
8 small onions
1 cup fresh sliced mushrooms
1 clove garlic, minced
bay leaf
pinch of thyme
½ cup brandy
½ bottle Gold Seal Champagne

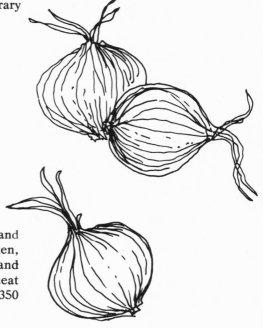

Cut chicken into pieces. Combine bacon, butter and onions in a casserole and cook at 400 degrees until the bacon is crisp and the onions brown. Add chicken, mushrooms, garlic, bay leaf and thyme. Return to 400 degree oven, cover, and cook another 30 minutes or until the chicken is brown. Skim excess fat, heat brandy and pour over chicken and ignite. Add Champagne, reduce heat to 350 and cook until done. Serves 6.

POULET SAUTÉ SEC

Sec is the French word for "dry." And one of the best chicken recipes the French love to serve at home is Poulet Sauté Sec. The original recipe from France called for Champagne and that's what we'll use.

"Champagne is one of the elegant extras of life."
Charles Dickens, (1812-1870)

¼ cup flour
1 Tbsp. salt
1 tsp. black pepper
1-3 lb. chicken, cut up
4 Tbsp. butter
¼ cup onions, chopped fine
2 Tbsp. parsley, minced
Pinch of thyme
Pinch of basil
½ cup Champagne
¼ lb. mushrooms, sliced and
   sautéed in butter

Put the flour, salt and pepper in a plastic bag and coat the chicken pieces. Melt the butter in a sauce pan and cook the chicken until brown all over. Add onions, parsley, thyme, basil and Champagne. Cover and cook on the simmer for 30 minutes. Add mushrooms and cook another 10 minutes. Serves 4.

POULET A LA MAISON

Someone once called herbs a "pinch of love". What they meant was herbs have to be used with a bit of prudence or else the dish will be ruined. This is why a barbecue sauce with 30 ingredients will never taste as good as one with eight or ten: the flavors tend to cancel each other out. This herbed chicken uses fresh herbs but dried will suffice.

> *1-4 lb. fryer, cut up*
> *4 Tbsp. butter*
> *Salt & White Pepper to taste*
> *1 medium sized onion, diced*
> *½ cup dry Champagne*
> *½ cup chicken stock*
> *1 Tbsp. fresh squeezed lemon juice*
> *⅛ cup herbs, equal parts of parsley,*
>   *chives, basil and tarragon*

Melt half the butter in a large casserole. Add chicken, dust with salt & pepper and chopped onion. Add Champagne and stock. Cover and bake in a 325 degree oven for 45 minutes. Ten minutes before the chicken is done, melt the remaining butter in a saucepan, adding lemon juice and herbs. Cook 1 minute and pour over the chicken in the oven. Bake 10 minutes. Serves 6.

CHICKEN SAUTÉ

There are many little towns in the Champagne country of France where barnyard hens are quickly sautéed in Champagne. Here is one such recipe that takes about one half hour.

> *1-3 lb. fryer, cut up*
> *4 Tbsp. butter*
> *Salt & Pepper to your taste*
> *½ cup Champagne*
> *3 Tbsp. chopped parsley*

Brown the chicken in the melted butter in a saucepan. When evenly browned, add salt and pepper, turning the chicken parts as you season them. Lower heat and sauté 10 minutes. Add ½ the Champagne, cover and cook another 10 minutes. Remove the chicken to a warm platter. Add remaining Champagne and parsley to the pan, turn up the heat and cook for 1 minute. Pour over chicken. Serves 4.

CHICKEN SAUTÉ CYNTHIA

Perfected and submitted by Mr. Dick Bouchet of Christian Brothers.

2½ lb. chicken, boned and cut
*   into 4 pieces*
Flour
Butter
8 fresh mushrooms
½ onion, finely sliced
1 cup Christian Brothers Brut
*   Champagne*
1 cup half & half or heavy cream
1 Tbsp. Curacao
Juice from ½ lemon
20 seedless grapes
10 orange quarters
Truffles (optional)

Bone chicken and cut into 4 pieces: 2 leg and 2 breast sections. Season and dredge with flour. Sauté without browning in butter until nearly done, about 20 minutes. Add fresh mushrooms and onion and cook for 3 minutes more. Then add Champagne and whipping cream and let simmer until reduced by about half, and then blend in 1 tablespoon Curacao and the juice of one-half a lemon. Place on a platter and surround with grapes and orange quarters. Sprinkle with 1 tablespoon sliced truffles. Serves two.

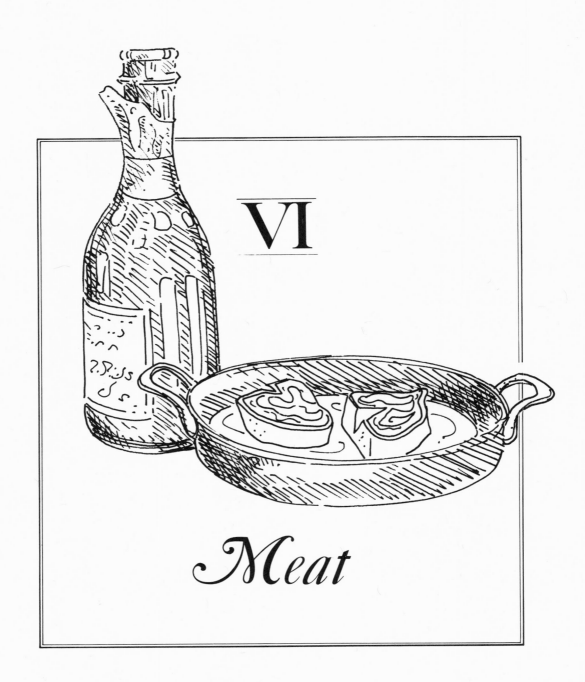

VI

Meat

Meat is man's oldest food staple. Whether it be beef, lamb, pork, ham or whatever, men have made a diet of meat in one form or another. And, man has always found beverages to wash down the meat.

Champagne and meat have much in common. Both have distinct tastes. Both mate well with each other in a variety of ways, in a variety of recipes, and both are enjoyed by man.

Twenty-five years ago the idea of drinking a white wine with red meat was frowned upon. Today, two of the most popular food and wine combinations are drinking Champagne with charcoal broiled steak and Cabernet Sauvignon with spit roasted chicken.

All meats, whether they are roasted in an oven, grilled over charcoal or wood, broiled or pan fried, are better if they are taken out of the refrigerator before they are cooked. A steak needs ½ hour of room temperature, while a large roast or leg of lamb needs 2-3 hours of room temperature.

When salting a roast, remember that it should be salted at least 10 minutes after it has been roasting, while grilled meats should be salted on the side first to be grilled and on the other side just before turning.

If you want to rub your roasts with oil before cooking, olive oil is best. It helps the color of the meat as well as the flavor.

And ideas about cooking have changed, too. Twenty-five years ago few chefs were deglazing pans with white wines. Today, many chefs prefer Champagne because it adds a new taste to the sauce.

HAM WITH A WINE VINEGAR SAUCE

The use of wine vinegars, which add to the piquant of a dish, is fast becoming the "in" ingredient. Wine vinegars add a certain zest to the sauce, a spicy zing, without additional calories.

4 Tbsp. butter
1 Tbsp. flour
Salt & Pepper to your taste
¾ cup chicken stock
½ cup Brut Champagne
2 Tbsp. Champagne vinegar
3 Tbsp. minced white onion
6 juniper berries, crushed
½ cup heavy cream (whipping)
*6 slices of cooked ham, cut ½
    inch thick*

In a saucepan, melt 1 Tablespoon of the butter and stir in the flour, salt and pepper. Add stock, Champagne, vinegar, and cook to the boil. Then add onions and juniper berries and cook over the simmer for at least 10 minutes. Strain through a fine sieve and add the cream. Mix well. Melt the remaining butter in a saucepan and sauté the ham slices so that they are heated through. Put the slices on a large platter, pour the sauce over them. Serves 6.

HAM IN CHAMPAGNE

Ham and Champagne have long been noted for their love of each other, as in this simple, but excellent recipe.

1 ham slice about one inch thick
1 bottle of Champagne
½ cup granulated sugar

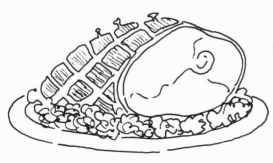

Place the ham slice in a glass baking dish. Pour in enough Champagne, just to cover the ham slice. Let this mixture marinate for at least 3 hours, turning the ham over after 1½ hours. Bake in a 325 degree oven for 30 minutes. Ten minutes before the ham is done, sprinkle the sugar over the ham and return it to the oven. When ham is done, take it out of the oven and place it under the broiler to caramelize the sugar, making sure the sugar does not burn. Serves 4.

HAM WITH TOMATO SAUCE

There's nothing like fresh tomatoes to enhance the flavor of a dish. And then add some Champagne, cream, and onions.

1½ cups Champagne
½ cup onions, minced
3 cups beef stock
¾ cup tomatoes, peeled, seeded and diced fine
¼ tsp. freshly ground white pepper
¼ tsp. basil
2 Tbsp. flour
1 cup heavy cream (whipping)
2 Tbsp. butter
6 slices of cooked ham, each ½ inch thick

Cook onions in Champagne until the liquid is reduced by half. Add stock, tomatoes, pepper and basil. Bring to the boil, reduce heat to the simmer and cook for one hour. Purée the mixture. Return to clean saucepan. Mix flour and cream and add to the pan. Keep stirring so the sauce will not burn. Cook over the simmer for 10 minutes. Melt butter in saucepan, add ham slices and quickly sauté them until they are heated through and slightly brown. Place slices on a heated platter and pour the sauce over them. Serves 6.

CHAMPAGNE SAUCE

The Taylor Wine Company, Inc. has been making wines since 1880 and Champagne since 1941. From their kitchens comes this recipe for glazing ham.

⅔ cup light brown sugar
2 Tbsp. cornstarch
2 tsp. grated orange rind
1 cup fresh orange juice
2 cups Taylor New York Extra Dry or Brut Champagne

Combine first four ingredients in a sauce pan. Heat, stir constantly. Boil one minute. Remove from heat, add Champagne. Reheat, but do not boil. NOTE— This sauce is used to glaze the ham as well as to serve with the ham.

SAUERKRAUT, PORK AND CHAMPAGNE

Buffets lend themselves to a great many dishes. It seems that the gourmet can have several courses before he/she can return to sample again. And if the Champagne is flowing, the buffet can become the supreme delight. This next recipe is for six, but after you see the ingredients, you might want to invite more people.

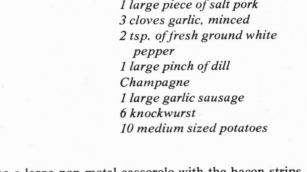

6-8 slices of blanched bacon
4 lbs. of washed sauerkraut
1 lb. loin of pork, boned and tied
6 pig's knuckles
1 large piece of salt pork
3 cloves garlic, minced
2 tsp. of fresh ground white
  pepper
1 large pinch of dill
Champagne
1 large garlic sausage
6 knockwurst
10 medium sized potatoes

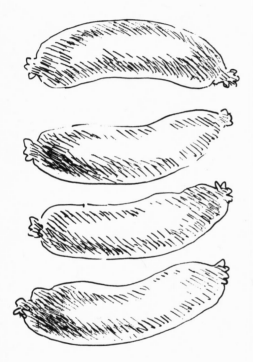

Line a large non-metal casserole with the bacon strips. Spread the sauerkraut over the bacon. Wipe the loin of pork and lay it in the middle of the sauerkraut. Add the pig's knuckles, salt pork, garlic, pepper and dill. Add Champagne to cover the ingredients. Cover and simmer for 4 hours. Add garlic sausage and cook another 15 minutes. Now add the knockwurst and cook another 20 minutes. In a separate pan boil the unpeeled potatoes for 30 minutes. Using a large platter, arrange the sauerkraut in the center. Slice the pork loin, sausages and salt pork and put them on top of the sauerkraut. Surround them with the boiled potatoes. Serves 6 healthy appetites.

PORK WITH RED CABBAGE

1 large head of red cabbage
4 Tbsp. butter
2 lb. loin of pork
Salt & Pepper to your taste
2 Tbsp. sugar
1 cup dry Champagne

Core the cabbage and discard any wilted leaves. Cut the cabbage as for slaw. Melt the butter in a large pan and brown the pork all over. Put the cabbage around the pork and add the remaining ingredients. Cover tightly and simmer for 2 hours. When cooked, remove the meat, slice it. Put the sliced meat on a heated platter and surround it with the cabbage. Serves 4.

SAUCISSON DE PORC AU CHAMPAGNE

Some years ago when I was in France, I stopped at a little restaurant in Pouilly-Fuisse. It was here that I first tasted the delightful dish of pork sausages cooked in Pouilly-Fuisse wine. The owner of Au Pouilly-Fuisse wouldn't give me the recipe, but I have re-created it here using Champagne.

1 Tbsp. butter
1 lb. pork sausages
1 cup natural Champagne
1 cup chicken stock
1 medium onion, minced
2 cloves garlic, minced
Herb bouquet composed of equal parts of white peppercorns, thyme, basil and marjoram tied in a small piece of cheese-cloth
1 Tbsp. tomato paste
Salt & Pepper to your taste
1 Tbsp. fresh parsley, minced

In an enameled cast iron pan, melt the butter and lightly brown all the sausages. Add all remaining ingredients, except the parsley and bring to the boil. Reduce heat to the simmer and cook for 30 minutes, or until the sausages are done. With a slotted spoon, remove the sausages to a warm platter. Reduce the cooking liquid to half over fairly high heat. Correct the seasoning, strain and pour over the sausages. Sprinkle with minced parsley. **NOTE:** Many restaurants serve this dish with a variety of mustards. Serves 4-6.

PORC A LA REINE

4 pork chops, ½ inch thick, trimmed of all fat
1 Tbsp. clarified butter
½ Tbsp. cornstarch
½ cup chicken stock
½ cup Champagne
20 slices of onion, ¼ inch thick
Pinch of tarragon
Salt & White pepper to your taste

Sauté chops in butter until brown on both sides. Remove chops and discard all the fat except one tablespoon. Mix cornstarch with stock and stir until smooth. Add to pan along with the Champagne. Return chops to the pan, top with onions and tarragon, salt & pepper. Cover and cook 40 minutes on the simmer. Serves 4.

THIRSTY AMERICANS

In 1979, California shipped some 20,000,000 gallons of Champagne to the market.

Another way of looking at it, is that this figure represents about a gallon of Champagne for every man, woman and child in California.

Or, it is 100,000,000 fifth bottles of Champagne.

Or, it is 833,333 plus cases of 12 fifths of Champagne,

Or, Americans like California Champagne.

LAMB PROVENÇAL

This is one of the most delicate dishes that marries red meat with white wine. A nice leg of lamb, a bottle of Champagne, and several cloves of unpeeled garlic and your mouth is ready for a great taste treat.

1 leg of lamb, about 4-5 lbs.
8-10 cloves of garlic, unpeeled
1 bottle of Brut Champagne
Salt & Pepper to your taste

Trim the skin or fat from the leg so that most of the red meat is showing. In a roasting pan large enough to hold the leg, put in a trivet about 2-3 inches high. Set the lamb on the trivet. Add the garlic cloves, about ¾ of the Champagne and sprinkle the leg with salt and pepper. Place the leg in a 325° oven. Baste the leg every 10 minutes. When the meat thermometer says done, remove lamb. Skim off fat from the basting juices. Slice the lamb and serve with juices and garlic. Serves 6.

ROAST LAMB IN CHAMPAGNE SAUCE

Created in Reims, France, this roast lamb in Champagne sauce almost cooks itself. One caution: The recipe calls for beef broth and if you have some homemade beef broth, so much the better. If you use canned beef broth, add 1 Tablespoon tomato puree. Cook for 5 minutes over the simmer and then use.

3-4 lb. leg of lamb, with the skin
*   removed and trimmed of all fat*
Salt & Black pepper to your taste
⅓ cup of flour
4 Tbsp. butter
¼ cup beef broth
1½ cups Champagne
½ cup grated onion
1 clove garlic, minced

Mix the salt, pepper and flour together and rub the leg of lamb with it. Place in a roasting pan with the butter and roast at 450° for 20 minutes. Add remaining ingredients and roast at 350° for about 2 hours or until the meat thermometer registers the lamb done. Skim fat from sauce and serve separately. Serves 6.

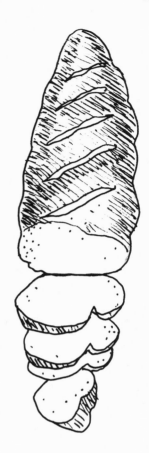

FILET MIGNON AVEC CHAMPAGNE

Champagne is an excellent deglazing agent. Anything that has been sautéed renders small brown particles which when deglazed with Champagne, stock and minced onions, creates an instant sauce. See how this recipe is improved by such an addition.

> *4 Tbsp. butter*
> *4 fillets of beef, cut one inch thick*
> *Salt & Pepper to your taste*
> *4 slices of French bread, sautéed*
> *2 Tbsp. white onions, minced*
> *½ cup dry Champagne*
> *½ cup beef stock*

In a sauce pan melt 3 Tablespoons of butter and sauté the fillets over high heat 3 minutes on each side. Season with salt and pepper and place on the bread. Keep warm. Deglaze the pan by adding remaining ingredients and reduce to half. Pour over fillets. Serves 4.

VEAL CHOPS FARMER STYLE

Veal is gaining popularity in the United States. In fact, there are several "veal farms" in the United States, something unheard of 25 years ago. While veal is expensive, it is well worth the effort to go the extra mile.

> *6 loin or rib veal chops, ¾ inch*
> *   thick*
> *Salt & Pepper to your taste*
> *½ cup flour*
> *6 slices of bacon*
> *3 Tbsp. butter*
> *12 small boiling onions*
> *¼ cup Brut Champagne*
> *¾ cup chicken stock*

Mix the flour, salt and pepper and dip the chops, coating them well. In a saucepan, fry the bacon until crisp. Drain, pour off fat, dry bacon and crumble it. In the same saucepan, melt the butter and lightly brown the onions all over. Remove onions. In the butter remaining in the pan, sauté the chops until brown. Add onions, bacon, Champagne and stock. Cook covered on simmer for 35-40 minutes. Serves 6.

BEEF IN CHAMPAGNE

If you are big with buffets, here is a dish that your friends will be coming back for more and more.

3 Tbsp. clarified butter or oil of
* your choice*
2 lbs. of beef cut in ¾ inch
* chunks*
Salt & Black pepper to your taste
¾ cup chopped onions
1 clove garlic, minced
1½ cups peeled, seeded and
* diced tomatoes*
2 Tbsp. flour
1½ cups chicken stock
1 cup Extra Dry Champagne
½ lb. mushrooms, quartered
2 Tbsp. butter

Heat the oil in a heavy saucepan and brown the beef all over. Add salt, pepper, onions, garlic and tomatoes. Mix well and cook 2 minutes. Sprinkle in flour and stir again. Now add stock and Champagne, cover and cook over the simmer for 1 hour. In a separate saucepan, sauté the mushrooms in the butter for 3 minutes and add to the beef. Cook the mixture another 10 minutes. Serves 6.

BEEF RIBS

Many butchers have to bone out beef ribs to make rolled roasts. Often times these ribs are sold to people who are tired of spare ribs and like a change of pace. Ask your butcher to save you some beef ribs, about 3 per person is ample, the next time you visit him. And then try this recipe.

12 beef ribs, meaty and well
* trimmed of fat*
¾ cup tomato catsup
¾ cup Brut Champagne
Salt & Pepper to your taste

Cook the beef ribs over oak wood or charcoal or broil them under the broiler. Mix the catsup and Champagne, add salt and pepper and stir well. About half way through the cooking process, start basting the ribs with the sauce. If the catsup starts to brown, lower the broiler. Turn the ribs over several times, each time basting them. Total cooking time is about 30 minutes, depending upon how much meat your butcher leaves on the ribs. Serves 4.

BEEF & CLAM STEW

When is a stew not a stew? When it is a ragout, or matelote, or meurette, or cassoulet, or jambalaya, or gumbo, or pot au feu or garbare . . . .

Confused? You should be because the wonderful world of stews is confusing.

There is no clear definition of a stew. It's all borderline. In the beginning there was a soup: clear, brown and soothing. Then someone added meat. Later another added vegetables. Later another added fish, then . . . . well you know what happened. Soups became thicker, heavier and began to be a four course meal in a pot.

Herewith is an unusual stew because it mixes meat and shellfish. It is probably Hispanic in origin, but then who really knows.

> *2 lbs. lean beef, cut into ½ inch*
>   *cubes*
> *3 Tbsp. salad oil*
> *2 large onions, sliced thin*
> *2 cloves garlic, minced*
> *3 large tomatoes, peeled, seeded*
>   *and chopped*
> *1-6 oz. can tomato paste*
> *2 cups dry Champagne*
> *Salt & Pepper to your taste*
> *2 dozen clams, washed and well*
>   *scrubbed*
> *2 Tbsp. parsley, minced*

Dry beef cubes. Heat oil in a large 5 quart kettle. Brown the cubes and with a slotted spoon remove to a warm plate. Add onions and garlic to the kettle and sauté until onions are tender. Return beef to kettle. Add tomatoes, tomato paste, Champagne, and salt and pepper. Bring to the boil, reduce to the simmer and cook for 1 hour or until the beef is tender. Add clams and cook another 15 minutes. Discard those clams which do not open. Add parsley, mix well. Serves 6.

FILET DE BOEUF A LA CHAMPAGNE ROSE

> *4 small filets of beef, ½ inch*
>   *thick*
> *4 Tbsp. butter*
> *Salt & Black pepper to your taste*
> *1 Tbsp. minced parsley*
> *1 tsp. dried rosemary, crushed*
> *1 tsp, dried thyme, crushed*
> *¾ cup Rose Champagne*

Sauté the filets in half the butter until rare. Remove and keep warm. Add salt & pepper, parsley, thyme and sauté so the flavors marry well, about two minutes, stirring well. Add Champagne and deglaze the pan. Add remaining butter and when melted, pour over the filets. Serves 4.

TRIPE CHAMPENOIS

From Ken Hoop of Wine Appreciation Guild we have an economical variety meat dish: "Many Spanish and Italian recipes for tripe incorporate the use of tomatoes. This dish is a modified recipe from France and was inspired by my dear friend Mrs. Gina Tauer, a native of that country."

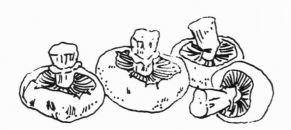

2-2½ lbs. Honey Comb Tripe
2 Tbsp. olive oil
2 Tbsp. butter
1 medium size onion, chopped
2 cloves garlic, crushed
1 Tbsp. flour
1 cup chicken broth
2 cups Champagne
1 bay leaf
¼ tsp. dried thyme
Dash cayenne pepper (optional)
Salt & Pepper
2 Tbsp. butter
¼ lb. fresh button mushrooms
2 egg yolks
2-3 Tbsp. brandy
Several drops lemon juice
1 Tbsp. parsley, chopped
2 Tbsp. butter

Wash tripe and cut into strips ½"x2". Place in large pot and cover with water. Bring to the boil and cook for 20 minutes. Drain and rinse well. Return to pot. Cover with fresh water and again boil for 20 minutes. Drain and rinse well with warm water. (This process eliminates the formation of foam in the preparation.) In the pot sauté the onion and garlic in the 2 Tbsp. butter and olive oil until lightly golden. Sprinkle with flour and mix well. Add chicken broth and Champagne. Mix and simmer for 5 minutes. Add drained tripe, bay leaf, thyme, cayenne (if desired) and salt and pepper to taste. Cook, uncovered, for 1½ to 2 hours until tender. In a pan, sauté mushrooms in 2 Tbsp. butter and add to tripe. Beat egg yolks and mix with brandy. Add to tripe and mushrooms. Mix well over low heat to bind. Add remaining butter, parsley and lemon juice. Mix and serve piping hot. Serves 4.

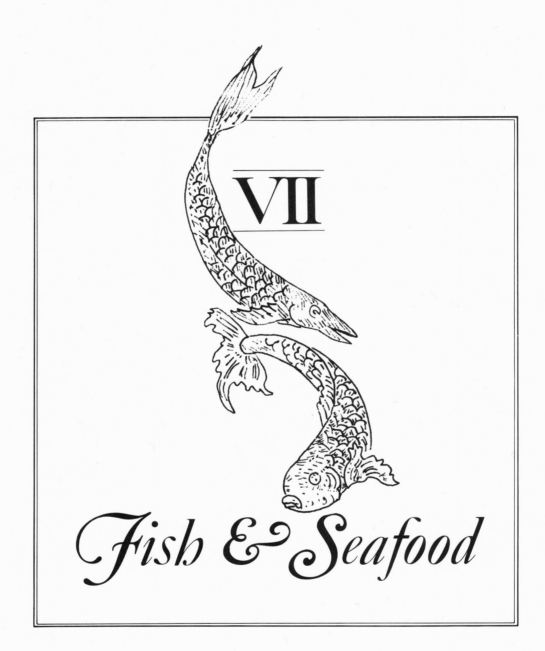

VII

Fish & Seafood

I first fell in love with Champagne and seafood more than 25 years ago on a remote sand dune in the area of Grand Isle, Louisiana. My father, uncle and I had been fishing for the Pacific Ocean speckled trout. They measured 10 to 12 inches and we hauled them in by the dozen. I even caught two fish on one hook, the first and last time that ever happened to me.

In those days, there were no limits. You caught what you could eat and then froze the rest, and if you felt generous, you gave some to your friends.

I had tired of drinking beer. I bought some California Champagne. After the trout had been cleaned and sautéed in butter, I washed the trout down with ice cold Champagne. I can still hear the ocean, taste the trout and savor the Champagne.

To this day, I still prefer Champagne with seafood. Mussels, scallops, oysters, clams; they all smell of the sea and marry well with a dry Champagne. But I can't exclude shrimp, crab, sole, salmon, bass and lobster.

Before we begin with our recipes, here are two bouillons in which fish is poached. One is made with the fish trimmings and the other is a simple bouillon without fish trimmings. After the fish is poached, it is removed, set in a warm oven and the bouillon reduced to make a sauce.

CHAMPAGNE COURT BOUILLON

2 cups dry Champagne
2 cups water
½ cup onions, minced
½ cup carrots, minced
4 black peppercorns, crushed
1 clove
1 bay leaf
1 stalk celery
3 sprigs parsley
1 tsp. salt

Combine all ingredients in a large sauce pan. Bring to the boil and simmer for 30 minutes. Strain. NOTE— If you want a slight fish taste to the bouillon, add 1 cup of clam juice and eliminate 1 cup of water.

FISH COURT BOUILLON

½ lb. fish trimmings (heads and
*   bones)*
1 cup dry Champagne
1 quart of water
2 sprigs of parsley, left whole
1 medium onion, stuck with
*   three cloves*
4 black peppercorns, crushed
1 tsp. salt
½ bay leaf
Pinch of dried tarragon
Slice of lime

Combine all ingredients in a large saucepan, bring to the boil and then simmer for 30 minutes. Strain.

POISSON EN PAPILLOTE

It was the Greek bandits who are said to have invented paper bag cookery. By using heavily oiled parchment paper to cook their foods in, the cooking aromas stayed concealed and couldn't lead their enemies to their camps.

Little was known or written about paper bag cookery until 1901 when the French balloonist Albert Santos-Dumont visited New Orleans and dined at Antoine's. Jules Alciatore, son of the founder Antoine Alciatore, wanted to prepare something special for the visiting Frenchmen. From a Greek cookbook he took a recipe using parchment paper and topped it with shrimp and crabmeat sauce. He folded the paper and baked it and thus was born "Pampano en Papillote."

Today, most people use aluminum foil in cooking "en papillote". The best foil is the heavy duty kind. It folds and seals better than the regular foil. The following recipe is for almost any kind of fish. Remember to allow 3-4 inches of extra foil on all sides of the fish. This will insure a complete fold plus extra air space above the fish.

*1 medium sized fish or a piece
    of fish
1 sheet of heavy duty aluminum
    foil, 3-4 inches wider than the
    fish
Salt & White pepper to your taste
1 thin slice of lemon
1 half bay leaf
2 Tbsp. butter
3 Tbsp. Champagne*

Place the fish on the foil. Raise the sides of the foil, making sure the corners are tight. Salt and pepper the fish. Add lemon, bay leaf, butter and Champagne. Fold foil around fish tightly, leaving a small air space above the fish. Bake at 400 degrees in the oven for 30 minutes or over the barbecue for 40 minutes. Serves 1.

NATURAL DISINFECTANT
Christopher Columbus knew the value of protecting his men from what we commonly call that scourge known as "Montezuma's revenge." To make sure that their intestinal equilibrium would remain stable during their dangerous voyage, he issued his men a daily ration of 2½ liters of red wine. Land ho!

CHAMPAGNE SALMON CREPES

1½ cups crepe batter (see batter
  recipe)

Crepe Batter:

1 cup flour
2 Tbsp. sugar
1 tsp. active dry yeast
4 egg whites
¾ cup milk
¼ cup butter

Combine flour, sugar and dry yeast. Add egg whites and milk, and beat to make a smooth batter. Melt butter in a medium sized skillet. When skillet is hot, pour a small amount of batter in and tip pan to spread batter over hot surface. Turn when bottom is brown and top of crepe is almost dry.

Make 4 crepes in 8″ pan, set aside.

2 Tbsp. butter
¼ cup chopped carrots
¼ cup chopped onions
1½ cup Lejon Champagne
½ tsp. chopped parsley
1 tsp. marjoram
¼ tsp. thyme
1 lb. salmon
1½ tsp. flour
1¼ tsp. butter
½ cup heavy cream
Salt and Pepper to your taste

"At the Pavillon they use better Champagne for cooking than most people ever drink with their food: the same Champagne that is served to the guests upstairs at seventeen dollars the bottle."

Joseph Wechsberg in
"Dining at the Pavillon"

Melt butter in saucepan. Saute onions, then carrots about 3 minutes each. Stir in 1¼ cups Lejon Champagne, add parsley, marjoram, thyme, salt and freshly ground pepper. Poach salmon for 15 minutes. Let cool in stock for another 15 minutes. Remove salmon and save liquid. Skin, fillet and flake fish. Set aside. Strain liquid and reduce to ¾ cup. In another saucepan, make a roux with the flour and butter. Pour in boiling reduced liquid, heating constantly. Warm cream and beat in by the spoonful, continuing to simmer until sauce is thick. Reduce remaining ¼ cup Lejon Champagne to about 1 tablespoon and add to sauce. Fill each crepe with flaked salmon and fold over twice. Cover in Champagne sauce and garnish with parsley. Serves 2.

STUFFED BASS WITH MUSSELS

Here is an outstanding recipe from the Christian Brothers Wine Harvest Luncheon held a few years ago. It is a little work, but well worth the effort.

1 striped bass (or mullet or rock
  fish) about 2½ pounds
Fish stock
½ pound fillet of sole
1 egg white
¾ cup heavy cream
½ tsp. salt
⅛ tsp. white pepper
Dash cayenne
6 cooked crayfish
1 (4/5 quart) bottle The Christian
  Brothers Brut Champagne
¼ cup chopped shallots
1 Tbsp. cornstarch
4 egg yolks. lightly beaten
6 mussels (poached)

Have fish man remove head and fins from fish, leaving tail on. Bone fish, cutting carefully at back, so skin is not broken. Use fish head and bones to prepare fish stock.   Place about half the sole at a time into blender, and blend until very finely chopped (or fish may be ground, using fine blade). Place sole in a bowl, set over ice water, and beat in egg white, stirring until well mixed. Gradually stir in ¼ cup cream. Add salt, pepper and cayenne. Shell crayfish, and remove tail meat. Cut in chunks and stir into the sole mixture. Stuff the fish with the sole mixture, and tie fish. Place in deep roasting pan. Strain fish stock, add champagne and shallots, and heat to boiling.   Pour over fish and poach in moderate over (350 degrees) about 30 minutes, basting often, until fish is cooked through and flakes easily at thickest part. Lift fish out onto serving platter and remove ties. Boil remaining stock rapidly until reduced to 2½ cups; strain. Stir cornstarch into remaining ½ cup cream. Add to the stock, and boil, stirring, until slightly thickened. Mix a little of the hot sauce into egg yolks. Combine with remaining sauce and cook a minute longer, without boiling, stirring briskly. Garnish fish with a little of the sauce, and the poached mussels. Pass remaining sauce. Makes 6 servings.

Fish Stock: Combine bones and head of fish with 1½ quarts water, 1 onion stuck with 2 cloves, 1 leek, 1 stalk celery, 1½ teaspoons salt, and ¼ teaspoon thyme. Heat to boiling, cover and cook 30 minutes. Strain, and add ¼ teaspoon powdered saffron.

To poach mussels: Turn ½ cup fish stock into small saucepan, and add mussels. Cover and simmer about 5 minutes, just until shells open.

HARVEY STEIMAN'S POACHED SOLE IN CHAMPAGNE

Harvey Steiman is the food and wine editor of the San Francisco Examiner and a lover of Champagne. Here is his favorite Champagne recipe, discovered when using the last few drops of some 1969 Schramsberg Blanc de Noir the day after some momentous occasion.

½ cup butter plus 1 tsp.
1 medium onion, sliced thin
2 fillets of sole, about 6 oz. each
½ cup Champagne
Salt & Pepper to your taste

Use 1 teaspoon of butter and butter the bottom of a baking dish. Lay the onion slices on the bottom of the baking dish. Put the sole on top of the onion, add the Champagne, salt and pepper and cover. Bake in a 400 degree oven for 12-15 minutes, depending upon the thickness of the sole. When cooked, carefully lift the fillets onto heated plates and cover with foil to keep them warm. Strain the liquid into a wide saucepan and reduce it to 2 tablespoons. Add remaining butter whisking to make a light sauce. Pour over fillets. Serves 2.

FEVER RELIEVER

Fevers are no fun. Serious fevers, that is those which last, should not be ignored and calls for medical advice.

Apart from the medications recommended and prescribed by the doctor, a good wine will help stimulate the patient's own biological defenses.

Dr. E.A. Maury, in his stimulating book, "Wine Is The Best Medicine" prescribes one bottle per day of either a dry or brut Champagne, taken in doses of one glass every hour. The good doctor explains:

"Champagne contains among other things two important elements for a feverish person: phosphorus, which is eminently stimulating and sulfur in its sulfate or potassium form, whose detoxifying action on the body has been established."

Thank you, Dr. Maury.

FILLETS OF SOLE WITH CHAMPAGNE

The Champagne News & Information Bureau in New York is the French Champagne industry's public relations arm in the United States. They have many excellent recipes and have shared this one with us.

12 fillets of sole
½ bottle of Brut Champagne
Salt & Pepper to your taste
1 small onion, minced
7 ounces of butter
6 Tbsp. heavy cream
4 egg yolks

Lay the fillets flat in a pan and cover with Champagne. Add salt, pepper, onion and one tablespoon of the butter. Bring slowly to the boil, reduce heat and let simmer for 6-8 minutes. When cooked, remove fillets to a warm platter and keep warm. Add remaining butter and let it melt off the heat. Mix the cream and yolks together and add enough cooking liquid until a medium thick sauce is obtained. Heat sauce below the boiling point. Pour over fillets. Serves 6.

LOBSTER ABSINTHE GOURMET

This is the only lobster recipe in this cookbook. It is the only one, not because lobster is expensive, which it is, but because in my opinion it is the best tasting lobster one can eat. I first encountered this ethereal dish at the old Chambord restaurant in New York on Third Avenue. Marcel was the head chef then and Paris and Rene were the maitres d'hotel. We were anticipating the chicken cooked in Champagne sauce, when Paris said that Marcel had received that afternoon a shipment of fresh live Maine lobsters. "Would you like to try our special lobster dish while the chicken is cooking?" he asked. "It will help pass some of the time away," he said. We all nodded yes and went on talking.

Sipping our Champagne, Paris brought out special neck napkins and tied them around our bodies. Then came the waiter with a silver tureen filled to the brim with a perfect white sauce in which little red claws and tails were protruding above the sauce. The aroma of cream, lobster and a special anise filled the table. For the next 15 minutes no one said a word. They were too awed to speak.

For some years after that I tried in vain to get the recipe, but failed. The closest recipe to the Chambord's is in Gourmet's first cookbook. It is called Lobster Absinthe Gourmet. I have used this recipe often and people ask for the recipe. I tell them to get the Gourmet Cookbook and read the recipe on page 256. The only change in the recipe I make is to cook the lobsters in Champagne instead of white wine. I think it tastes better that way.

> *3 medium sized live lobsters*
> *Brut Champagne*
> *10 sprigs of fresh tarragon or*
> *   1 Tbsp. dried*
> *4 Tbsp. butter*
> *2 Tbsp. flour*
> *Salt & White pepper to your taste*
> *1 Tbsp. each of dried tarragon*
> *   and chervil*
> *4 Tbsp. Absinthe, or Pernod,*
> *   heated*

Place the lobsters in a medium sized saucepan and cover them with the Champagne. Add tarragon and slowly bring the Champagne to the boil and let the lobsters simmer for 20 minutes. Cool them in the wine and when they are lukewarm, remove from the pan and cut their tails into 1½ inch pieces. Split the shell in half and crack the claws. Discard the black vein running from head to tail and small sack in back of the head. From the shells remove the green liver, or tomalley and the coral. Put them in a small saucepan and add 3 tablespoons of the butter and the flour. Heat this mixture gently, blend it into a smooth paste and add enough of the Champagne in which the lobsters were cooked to make a smooth sauce the consistency of light cream. Season lightly with salt and pepper and when the sauce is smooth add chervil and tarragon leaves. Place the lobster pieces in a large deep casserole, add the remaining tablespoons of butter and gently reheat. When the butter is foaming, pour over the lobster pieces the heated Absinthe or Pernod. Set aflame and when the spirit has burned out, add the sauce. Lift the lobster pieces gently with a spoon to let the sauce penetrate completely, cover the casserole and set it in a 225 degree oven for ten minutes to let the lobster become imbued with the various flavors. Serves 6.

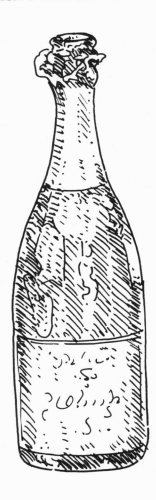

COQUILLES ST. JACQUES

At certain times of the year, scallop prices sink to new lows and that's the time when one of the most famous scallop dishes can be savored. It is always better to use fresh scallops for the taste is of the sea. However, frozen can still be an excellent substitute.

> *1½ lbs. scallops*
> *Sprigs of fresh thyme or ½ tsp.*
>   *dried*
> *1 bay leaf*
> *1 sprig parsley*
> *6 peppercorns, left whole*
> *Salt*
> *1 cup Champagne*
> *6 to 7 Tbsp. butter*
> *3 Tbsp. flour*
> *2 egg yolks*
> *1 tsp. lemon juice*
> *Parmesan cheese, freshly grated*

In a medium size saucepan, bring the scallops, thyme, bay leaf, peppercorns, salt and Champagne to the boil. Cover and simmer two minutes. Remove parsley, bay leaf and thyme. Reserve cooking liquid. Cool the scallops and cut into bite size pieces. Set aside. In another saucepan melt 2 Tbsp. of the butter and stir in the flour with a wire whisk. Take the pan off the heat and beat vigorously with the whisk while adding the remaining butter very gradually. When butter has been incorporated into the sauce, add the yolks by beating them into the sauce. Cool, and then add lemon juice. Spoon a little of the sauce in 6 large scallop shells. Divide the bite size scallop pieces evenly into the six shells. Spread the remaining sauce evenly over the six shells. Top with cheese. Bake 5 to 10 minutes or until bubbling in a 400 degree oven. Serves 6.

MON GENERAL

Even great generals got involved with Champagne. One such general was Mariano Guadalupe Vallejo. On April 25, the Alta California reported:

"An excellent champagne is offered for sale in this city (San Francisco) which certainly and irrefutably overthrows the oft-repeated assertion that California grapes can never produce a fine champagne. Gen. Vallejo has bottled a champagne, from the vintage of 1859, which, for body and flavor, will compare favorably with the imported brands of this universally fashionable beverage."

Gen. Vallejo's sparkling white wine was the best shown at the Sonoma Fair in October, 1862. After that, nothing was ever heard of it again.

SCALLOPS L'AIGLON

This dish is excellent as a first course. It also doubles as a light fish course if you want to serve both a fish and meat course as was once done years ago.

> *12 scallops, cut into three rounds*
> *7 Tbsp. butter*
> *4 Tbsp. fresh breadcrumbs*
> *Salt & White pepper to your taste*
> *½ cup Champagne*

Melt 4 Tbsp. of the butter in a sauce pan, adding 3 Tbsp. of the breadcrumbs, the Champagne and scallops. Cook 5 minutes. Divide the mixture evenly and put each portion into a scallop shell. Dot with remaining breadcrumbs and bake 15 minutes in a 325 degree oven. Serves 4.

SCALLOPS PIQUANT

Coquilles St. Jacques is a classic French dish. When prepared properly, with fresh sea scallops, unsalted butter, shallots, mushrooms and heavy cream the dish can be memorable. However, with the advent of cuisine minceur, the dish has fallen into disfavor by those who count calories and pounds.

Be that as it may, we have a splendid dish with scallops and Champagne, a dish that can be served as a first course or as a fish course and even an entrée. Naturally, you would serve Champagne with this dish.

> *1½ lbs. fresh scallops*
> *1½ Brut Champagne, plus 2*
> *   tablespoons*
> *½ Tbsp. cornstarch*
> *Paprika*
> *1 Tbsp. minced parsley*

Wash scallops. Bring the Champagne to the boil in a saucepan, add scallops and cook at the simmer for about 10 minutes. Remove the scallops, quarter them, keep warm. Mix the two tablespoons of Champagne with the cornstarch and when well mixed add to the scallop liquid. Heat, stir until a smooth sauce is obtained. Taste, correct seasonings. Divide the scallops evenly and put them in four scallop baking shells. Spoon the sauce over them, dust with paprika and parsley and heat at 450 degrees in the oven for 3 minutes. Serves 4.

SUPER SCALLOPS

If you like to broil seafood, scallops present something of a problem. Too many times the delicate flavor of the scallop is lost if it is broiled over charcoal or wood. You end up tasting the charcoal or wood and not the scallop. The best way to broil scallops is in the oven, basting them with an excellent Champagne marinade.

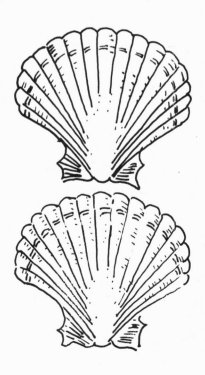

> *2 lbs. scallops*
> *1 cup olive oil*
> *1 cup Champagne*
> *1 tsp. dried tarragon*
> *Salt & White Pepper to your*
> *   taste*
> *¼ cup chopped parsley*
> *1 clove garlic, chopped*
> *1 small onion, chopped fine*

Wash scallops. In a large glass bowl, mix the remaining ingredients, soaking the scallops for 2 to 3 hours. Turn the scallops every half hour. Put 4 or 5 scallops on each wooden skewer and place on the broiler pan and broil about 4 inches from the heat. Turn frequently, basting them with the marinade. They should be cooked in 5 minutes. Serves 6.

Mussels abound throughout the United States. They are one of the most healthy of shellfish, are easy to obtain from hundreds of coasts in the temperate zone and are often abundant in estuaries where the fresh water meets the ocean.

Californians can harvest their own mussels between November 1 to April 30 without fear of paralytic shellfish poisoning. If you plan to harvest your own mussels or purchase them at a fish store, here are a few tips to remember.

1. Pick or buy mussels all the same size.

2. 1 quart of mussels contains 25 mussels each about three inches long.

3. Discard any mussel that when tapped, sounds hollow. Live mussels sound solid.

4. Use the mussels within two days after picking them and one day after buying them in the store.

Here are a few other tips that will come in handy when cooking mussels.

* Use a half a cup of liquid (Champagne) for every two quarts of mussels you plan to steam.

* After cooking the mussels the required time as called for in the recipe, discard all those mussels which have not opened. Unopened mussels are dead mussels.

MARINER'S MUSSELS

This is an old sailor's repast, which can again do double duty either as a main course or as a single course with plenty of crisp bread and Champagne.

> *3 quarts of mussels, scrubbed*
> *and trimmed of their beards*
> *1 clove garlic, crushed*
> *1 large onion, sliced thin*
> *A few sprigs of parsley*
> *4 Tbsp. butter*
> *Salt & fresh ground pepper to*
> *your taste*
> *½ cup dry Champagne*
> *4 additional Tbsp. of butter*
> *¼ cup chopped parsley*
> *¼ tsp. Tabasco sauce*

Put the first seven ingredients into a large pot and cook the mussels, tightly covered, for 5 to 7 minutes. Discard any mussel shells which do not open. Remove the mussels with a slotted spoon to a large tureen. Add remaining ingredients to the liquid. Taste and correct the seasonings. Divide the mussels evenly in soup bowls and pour over them some of the broth. Serves 4.

BUBBLY BATHERS

The 19th Century courtesan, Cora Pearl, once took a bath in 350 bottles of French Champagne. Not to be outdone, the late Marilyn Monroe did the same thing. Ms. Pearl drank the Champagne she bathed in; history doesn't record what Ms. Monroe did with the Champagne she bathed in.

SALADE DE MOULES AUX HERBES

One of the best cold mussel dishes I have ever eaten was served to me at Claude Darozze (1 ★) in Langon, France, just 20 miles south of Bordeaux.

Claude Darozze is one of the sons of Jean Darozze, of Darozze in Villeneuve-de Marsan (2 ★ ★). His brother, Francis Darozze is in Roquefort buying and personally bottling some of the finest Bas Armagnac in the world.

It was Francis who suggested that I dine at Claude Darozze and the first dish served was Salade de Moules aux Herbes.

4 lbs. three-inch mussels
1½ cups Champagne
⅓ cup mayonnaise
1 to 2 tsp. tomato catsup
2 Tbsp. whipping cream or crème
* fraiche*
1 Tbsp. fresh chopped parsley
1 Tbsp. fresh chopped chives
Lemon Juice

Scrub the mussels in cold water and remove their beards. Put the mussels in a large pot and pour the Champagne over them. Cover and cook over medium high heat for 5 to 7 minutes. Remove the mussels, reserve the liquid and discard the empty top shells. Arrange the filled shells on a platter and let cool. To prepare the herb butter, combine the mayonnaise and cream. Add the remaining ingredients plus some of the mussel liquid to make a sauce thick enough to coat the back of a spoon. Coat each of the mussels with the sauce. Serves 4.

MOULES A MA FAÇON

Here's another mussel recipe that can be used as an appetizer or by doubling the recipe, a delightful main course for lunch. Of course, you should serve a well chilled bottle of Champagne.

36 mussels, scrubbed and beards
* removed*
1 cup Champagne
¼ cup water
4 Tbsp. onion, minced
1 Tbsp. parsley, chopped
1 Tbsp. capers, chopped
1 tsp. dried tarragon
1 cup mayonnaise
1 hard cooked egg, minced

Put the mussels in a deep pot, pour the Champagne and water over them and cook 5 to 7 minutes. Discard any mussels whose shells do not open. Discard empty top shells. Cool mussels. Meanwhile, cook the onions, parsely, capers and dried tarragon in the Champagne liquid for 10 minutes. Cool. Add mayonnaise and egg. Cover the mussels with the mixture. Serves 4.

"I am drinking stars!"

Do you know who said that?

It was the man who put the stars into Champagne, the blind monk, Dom Perignon.

How farsighted, he was.

SHRIMPS LA TOUR

"I like garlic," the lady sitting next to me said. "But I like it in very small amounts."

There are many people like this lady. They like just a touch of garlic and that suits them fine. Here is such a recipe.

> 4 Tbsp. butter
> 4 Tbsp. olive oil
> 1 large clove garlic, peeled
> 2 lbs. raw, peeled and deveined
>   shrimp
> 2 Tbsp. parsley, minced
> ⅓ cup Champagne
> Salt & fresh ground black pepper

Heat the butter and oil with the garlic clove in a large saucepan. Cook garlic clove until just the edges start to brown. Off heat and discard garlic clove. Add shrimp and half the parsley and cook shrimp until they become pink. Test one and see if it is cooked. When done, remove shrimp with slotted spoon to a serving platter. Add Champagne and remainder of parsley to the juices in the pan. Bring to the boil and cook one minute. Pour sauce over the shrimp. Salt and pepper to taste. Serves 4 to 6.

SHRIMP IN HERBS

Some people don't want to be bothered cooking shrimp. They hate the peeling, deveining, cooking tasks that go with cooking your own shrimp. For those people who like to buy their shrimp cooked, here is a fast and easy entrée.

> 2 lbs. of peeled, deveined and
>   cooked shrimp
> ¼ lb. butter
> 1 clove garlic, minced
> 1 Tbsp. chopped chives
> 1 tsp. dried tarragon
> 1 Tbsp. chopped parsley
> ½ tsp. salt
> ½ tsp. fresh ground black
>   pepper
> ½ cup fine bread crumbs
> ½ cup Champagne

Arrange the cooked shrimp in a baking dish, spreading them evenly. Blend the softened butter with the remaining ingredients except the Champagne. Spread the mixture over the shrimp. Add the Champagne and put under the broiler for a few minutes or until the shrimp is heated through. Serves 4.

CHAMPAGNADE

They are white, pink and brown. They have been caught as close to a mile off the shore or as deep as 1,800 feet off the edge of the Continental shelf. They are classified by the United States by how many of them make up a pound. We call them shrimp.

Ever hear of the barber shrimp? This clever crustacean sets up his business in sea anemones and attracts lines of fish who want to get their fins and scales trimmed. And the terror of the tide, the modern "hit" man of shrimpdom, is the pistol shrimp. The demon of the deep has an extra long claw which resembles a pistol. He stuns his prey by noisily snapping it at them.

Shrimps and Champagne have a special thing about each other. And Valeria Furino, international food consultant and food designer for Paul Masson Vineyards has a special shrimp and Champagne recipe for you.

1 lb. shrimp, raw, peeled and
*   deveined*
Cornstarch
½ stick butter
⅛ cup olive oil
3 Tbsp. fresh chopped parsley
3 cloves garlic, minced
3 green and white onions,
*   minced*
Juice and rind of one lemon
Pinch of dill weed
Pinch of dried basil
Salt and pepper to taste
1 cup Paul Masson Brut
*   Champagne*

Pat the shrimp dry. Dust lightly with cornstarch and set aside. In a heavy pan, over medium heat, melt butter and olive oil, stir and add all other ingredients except the Champagne. Cook the mixture for 10 minutes, stirring occasionally. Add shrimp and cook 3 to 4 minutes, basting the mixture with the Champagne. Stir and finish cooking (2 more minutes). With a slotted spoon remove the shrimp to a serving platter and pour the Champagne sauce over the shrimp. Serves 4.

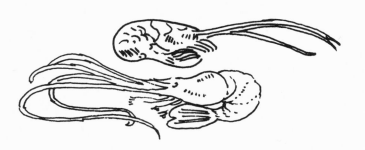

BAKED FILLET OF SOLE

Their last name is sole but they have many first names: Dover, Rex, Lemon, Gray, etc. They avoid combat, burrow themselves in the bottom of the cool ocean sands and eat only at night.

The sole is highly selective dietwise and that may account for their exquisite taste. Here is a recipe to enhance that delicate taste.

½ cup minced onions
2 Tbsp. minced parsley
¼ lb. mushrooms, sliced thin
½ cup dry bread crumbs
4 medium sized sole fillets
2 tsp. salt
5 grinds fresh white pepper
¾ cup dry Champagne
½ cup grated Mozzarella cheese

Butter a large baking dish. Scatter around the bottom of the dish one half the onions, parsley and mushrooms. Sprinkle the dish with half the bread crumbs. Lay the fillets over the vegetables. Cover the fillets with the remaining vegetables, salt and pepper and add the Champagne. Bake 10 minutes in a 375 degree oven. Mix the remaining bread crumbs with the cheese. Sprinkle over the fish and bake another 15 minutes. Serves 4 to 6.

VARIATIONS ON THE ABOVE RECIPE:

1. Substitute Parmesan cheese for the Mozzarella.
2. Add carrots, minced, to the vegetable list.
2. Add anise seeds for a liqueur taste.
4. Substitute cod, bass or snapper for the sole.

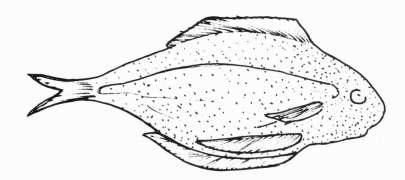

FILLET OF SOLE CHAMPAGNE

Here's another variation of the theme, but with a new approach.

12 oz. dry Champagne
1 cup thinly sliced mushrooms
½ cup grated onions
1 bay leaf
2 Tbsp. chopped parsley
⅓ cup heavy cream
Salt and pepper to your taste
3 lbs. sole fillets
⅓ cup Parmesan cheese

Put the first five ingredients into a sauce pan and cook on high until the mixture has been reduced by half. Remove the bay leaf and add the cream. Salt and pepper the fillets. Lay them in a baking dish and pour the sauce over them. Bake 20 minutes in a 375 degree oven. Serves 4 to 6.

SALMON IN GREEN CHAMPAGNE SAUCE

Fresh salmon has a special taste all its own. The salmon season is very long and fish markets always like to advertise the fact that their salmon is "fresh" and not "fresh frozen", whatever that means. When you can get fresh salmon, try this recipe from Charlie Olken, co-editor of Connoisseurs' Guide to California Wines.

4-6 oz. salmon steaks
2 cups Champagne
¼ cup parsley, chopped
¼ cup chives, chopped
2 Tbsp. green peppercorns
1 Tbsp. butter
2 Tbsp. heavy cream
Salt and pepper to taste

In a large sauce pan, poach the salmon steaks in Champagne, parsley, chives and green peppercorns. When the salmon is done (when it flakes, it's done), remove the steaks from the saucepan and keep warm in a slack oven. Reduce the poaching liquid to half its volume. Add butter and heavy cream. Mix well and cook one minute. Taste, correct seasonings and pour over salmon steaks, or serve separately in a sauceboat. Serves 4 to 6.

STEAMED CLAMS

Clams are probably one of the most sought after shellfish. Fresh caught and cooked properly, they can be one of nature's most delightful repasts.

24 fresh clams
Champagne
Melted butter

Wash and scrub the clams well, rinsing them in several changes of cold water to get rid of the sand. Check for clams with opened or damaged shells. If you find any, get rid of them. Put the clams in a large kettle or deep pot and pour in enough Champagne to make about ½ inch in the bottom. Cover, cook on high for 6 minutes or until the shells have opened. Discard any unopened shells. Strain the broth through a cheesecloth. Dunk the clams first in the clam broth and then in the melted butter. Serves 1.

STEAMED CLAMS ROMANO

Next is a variation of the above recipe. It has several names depending upon who you read. The most often used name for this dish is Steamed Clams Romano.

24 fresh clams
Champagne
1 Tbsp. butter
1 onion, peeled whole
2 sprigs of parsley
1 bay leaf
3 black peppercorns, left whole
Pinch of dried thyme
Melted butter

Follow the instructions for the Steamed Clam recipe, putting everything into the kettle or pot, except the melted butter. Cover and cook 6 minutes or until the shells have opened. Discard any unopened shells. Strain the broth through a cheesecloth. Dunk the clams first in the broth and then in the butter. Serves 1.

San Francisco's St. Mary's Hospital offers a special treat for mothers who have just given birth. The night before they are discharged from the hospital, the mothers and fathers are served a Champagne candlelight dinner. One expectant mother who had given birth at St. Mary's before, called the hospital to make sure the offer was still in effect. "I wouldn't have my baby anywhere else," she said.

LES HUITRES TIEDES au BLANC de POIREAUX et CHAMPAGNE

Jacky Robert, chef de cuisine at Ernie's Restaurant in San Francisco is one of the brightest and most talented chefs ever to grace the city Herb Caen calls "Baghdad by the Bay". He has slowly revised the menu to reflect the "nouvelle cuisine" yet still keeping some of the favorite dishes for the Ernie regulars. His credentials are impressive: Prunier's in Paris (2★★) and Maxim's of Paris (3★★★). M. Robert is using California Champagne in much of his cooking. Here is his recipe for a splendid first course with blue point oysters, cream and California Champagne.

White of 4 leeks, cut julienne
12 Blue Point oysters
1 shallot, minced
½ lb. butter
2 cups dry Champagne
Oyster juice
Salt & Cayenne pepper
4 cups whipping/ heavy cream
1 tsp. lemon juice

Blanch the leeks in boiling salted water. Open the oysters, reserving the juice. Saute the shallots in the butter and when soft add Champagne. Reduce the mixture by ⅔ its original volume. Add reserved oyster juice. Season mixture with salt and cayenne pepper. Poach the oysters in the reduction. While the oysters are poaching, heat the oyster shells in the oven. After two minutes of poaching, remove the oysters and place in the heated shells. Put them back in the warm oven. Reduce the remaining juice by half, add cream and reduce again to a thick consistency. Add lemon juice. Stir, divide the sauce evenly for the 12 oysters. Top with leeks. Serves 2.

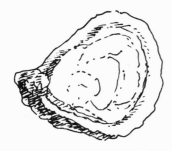 

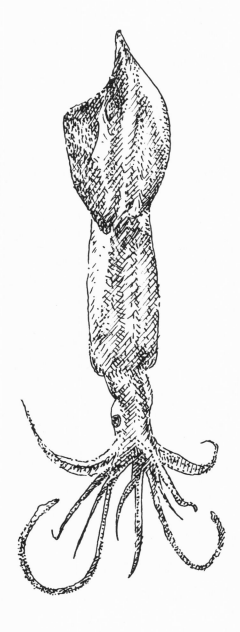

Calamari (or Squid) have been a delightful part of the cuisine of the Mediterranean area for centuries. The texture and wonderfully delicate flavor of this fish are very similar to those of Abalone. Preparation is not as difficult as it may at first appear, and actual cooking time is very short. Dressing the Calamari is easily done with just a pair of kitchen shears.

Remove the head by cutting the tendons connecting the body and the head. Cut the tentacles closely at their base separating them in one piece from the head. Discard the head. Place your finger in among the tentacles and press toward the cut edge. A small fleshy ball will then protrude which contains the small beak of the squid. This is easily removed and discarded. With the shears, cut the body lengthwise along the side of the spine. The celluloid-like spine and the entrails are easily detached with your fingers. Remove and discard. You will now have a flat piece of clean flesh and a small bunch of tentacles for cooking. There are about 10 to 12 small calamari to the pound.

The texture of Calamari is somewhat resilient. If you wish to tenderize the flesh, simply pat dry with paper towel and pound flat with a wooden mallet or back of a wooden spoon.

CHAMPAGNE CALAMARI

1 lb. Calamari
2 eggs
¾ cup seasoned dry bread
  crumbs
2 Tbs. flour
4 Tbsp. butter
2 Tbsp. olive oil
3 Tbsp. Champagne
½ fresh lemon
1 Tbsp. chopped parsley

Dress the Calamari as described above. Lay out and pound flat to tenderize as above. Beat eggs in a bowl. In separate bowl mix bread crumbs and flour. Dip pieces of calamari first in eggs then in crumbs to coat. Melt butter and oil in large pan. Over medium-high heat sauté calamari until golden brown (about 5 minutes), stirring and turning quickly and often. When golden brown add Champagne and cook 2 or 3 minutes longer. Remove to warm platter, squeeze lemon over all and sprinkle with parsley. Serve immediately. Serves 2 or 3.

VIII

Vegetables

The first newspaper food and wine column I ever wrote appeared on the food pages of the Chicago Daily News in June, 1962. It was a very bold move for the conservative Daily News to appoint a man to write about food and wine, especially since no man had ever been appointed to such a position.

Entitled "Gentlemen Chef", my column was directed to the male readers of the Chicago Daily News. More and more men were stepping into the kitchen in the late 1950's and early 1960's and the Daily News felt that its food pages should editorially address themselves to this change. The column caught on and within two months after its appearance, the Daily News syndicated it and within three months, it appeared in forty newspapers with a circulation of 3,500,000. By today's standards, forty newspapers for a column may not seem like a lot, but thank heaven there were forty newspaper editors in America who could see and spot the trend of "men moving into the kitchen."

While the column was a success, it was not without its problems. Everything I wrote was inspected and tested by the newspaper's kitchen staff. Even though I had tested recipes and had served the results to my friends, they still wanted to "try" them. After three months of CIA scrutiny, they finally trusted me. Testing days were over and I could get on with the business at hand.

Not much has changed since those early food and wine writing days. The most popular vegetable associated with Champagne is still sauerkraut. Today there is a brand of sauerkraut that is packed in Champagne. Instead of adding water to the pickling process, these people have added Champagne to give the sauerkraut a softer, more distinct taste.

But every recipe doesn't have to be made with sauerkraut. Marilou Heck, wife of Gary Heck, executive vice president of F. Korbel and Bros. in Guerneville, has been experimenting with Korbel Champagne and cabbage. She simply calls it:

ELEGANT CABBAGE

1 small head of cabbage, about
*   1½ to 2 lbs.*
¼ cup oil (olive or peanut)
⅔ cup Korbel Champagne
1 tsp. lemon pepper

Remove core and outer leaves of the cabbage. Shred. Put the oil in a large skillet over high heat and when oil is almost at the sizzle, add cabbage. Stir several times. Add half the Champagne. Stir and cover. Cook for five minutes, removing the lid several times to stir the mixture. After five minutes add remaining Champagne. Stir, cover and cook another five minutes, or until the liquid has evaporated. Do not scorch. Serves 6.

Mrs. Heck has several suggestions for variations on the above theme:
1. When adding the last half of the Champagne, add ¼ cup brown sugar.
2. When shredding the cabbage, add 1 cup diced apple.
3. For extra color, use red cabbage and Korbel Sparkling Burgundy.

MY FAVORITE SAUERKRAUT

AH, THE ENGLISH!

A 200 year old English recipe for a "fricassee of mushrooms" calls for 1 cup of Champagne, ½ cup or less of beef broth, butter mixed with flour, onions, herbs and mace. Simmer fresh mushrooms in this for 15 minutes. Just before serving, add mixed egg yolks and cream and heat briefly. Squeeze some orange or lemon juice over the top and serve.

From *Favorite Recipes of California Winemakers*, published by The Wine Appreciation Guild.

A few years ago, some friends and I got into an argument about what is the best way to serve sauerkraut. After several hours of constant chatter, I left the group thinking how foolish it was to argue the point. Tastes vary. No two people have the same tastes. With this thought in mind, I began playing detective, trying to find clues that would make up sauerkraut that I liked. You may not like it, but at least it will give you a point to start and search out your own favorite recipe.

2 lb. sauerkraut, well washed
3 whole garlic cloves, peeled
1½ tsps. fresh ground black
*   pepper*
8 crushed juniper berries
1 cup Champagne
1 cup chicken stock

Put everything into a large non-metal Dutch oven. Bring to the boil, reduce to simmer and cook one hour. Serves 6.

CHERVIL ASPARAGUS

They are sometimes called "sparrow grass," considered to be a cure for heart trouble, dropsy and toothaches. We call them asparagus, but the Romans thought they cured bee stings.

Asparagus are a member of the lily-of-the-valley family. The best months for asparagus are from March through June, but in most years those thin little delightful asparagus are available during the last two weeks in February.

1 lb. fresh asparagus, washed,
*   tough ends cut off*
3 Tbsp. sweet butter, melted
¼ cup dry Champagne
Salt & White Pepper to your
*   taste*
5 Tbsp. grated Mozzarella
1 large pinch chervil

Cook the asparagus in salted water to cover for 10 minutes. Test with a fork and when almost done, remove and drain. Place in a baking dish. Add butter, Champagne, salt & pepper, cheese and chervil. Bake in a 425° oven for 10 minutes, or until the cheese is slightly brown. Serves 6.

BROCCOLI FLEURIE

Broccoli is one of the oldest members of the cabbage family. The Greeks and Romans were eating broccoli more than 2,000 years ago. It wasn't until 1939 that broccoli became an established crop in the United States. The best way to cook broccoli is to steam it and then sauce it.

1 large bunch of broccoli, cut into
*   bite size pieces*
3 egg yolks
1 tsp. cornstarch
½ cup Champagne
1 Tbsp. lime juice
3 Tbsp. melted butter
Salt to taste
Cayenne pepper to taste

Steam the broccoli for 15 minutes in 1 cup of water. Meanwhile, beat the yolks in the bottom of a double boiler or a deep sauce pan. Add cornstarch, Champagne, lime juice and butter. Cook very slowly over low heat and stir constantly. The sauce should thicken in 2 to 3 minutes. Pour sauce over broccoli. Serves 4.

SPARKLING BAKED BEANS

Everytime I hear about or eat baked beans, I think of my friend Jacques Goux, general manager of Chateau de Malliac, in Montreal du Gers in France. Mr. Goux and his firm make some of the finest Armagnac in France. It has just become available in the United States. Mr. Goux spent some of his youth working in Boston, and fell in love with Boston Baked Beans. He told me this story in 1975 when I visited him and was allowed to taste the exquisite 1893 vintage Armagnac of which there are only 400 bottles in existence. I repaid him that privilege by sending him a special case of Boston Baked Beans.

I don't know how many recipes there are for baked beans, Boston or not. But I know that of the many hundreds I have tasted, none is better, in my opinion than the following recipe.

4 medium onions, sliced thin and
*   minced*
3 Tbsp. butter
2 cans (16 oz.) of your favorite
*   baked beans*
1 cup grated Cheddar cheese
4 Tbsp. Champagne

Sauté onions in butter until soft. Add remaining ingredients. Mix gently. Transfer to an ovenproof baking dish and bake at 325 for 40 minutes. Serves 6. NOTE: You can substitute any cheese for the Cheddar.

CHAMPAGNE AND ONIONS

24 small white onions, peeled
¾ cup Champagne
6 Tbsp. butter
½ bay leaf
1 large parsley sprig
Large pinch dried thyme
Salt and pepper to your taste
Chopped parsley (optional)

In a sauce pan with a tight fitting cover, put in the onions, Champagne, half of the butter, bay leaf, parsley sprig and thyme, salt and pepper. Cover and cook at the simmer for 45 minutes, or until the onions are tender. Add remaining butter. Just before serving, remove parsley sprigs and pour mixture onto a heated serving platter. Top with chopped parsley. Serves 4.

The French Champagne firm of Gosset dates back to 1584 thus making it the oldest wine house in Champagne.

The largest producer of sparkling wines by the methode champenoise is Codorniu in San Sadurni de Noya, just a few miles from Barcelona, Spain. They produced some 36,000,000 bottles of sparkling wine last year and have been winegrowers since 1551.

CHAMPAGNE ARTICHOKES

Artichokes are one of the vegetable kingdom's great gifts to mankind. So popular are these little thistles that many people have taken to growing them in their backyards. They mature quickly and you have the happy choice of picking them when you want to and not having to accept the grocer's choice.

The possible combinations of wines and vegetables are endless. Here is one such combination for your pleasure.

6 small artichokes, about the size
*   of a tennis ball.*
1 Tbsp. olive oil
1 clove garlic, minced
1 onion, minced
Pinch of tarragon
1 Tbsp. salt
1 cup Brut Champagne

Destem the artichokes, cut off the tops, about halfway, and remove some of the outer leaves. In a large pot big enough to hold the artichokes upright, put in the oil, garlic, onion, tarragon and salt. Stand the artichokes upright. Pour over the Champagne over them. Cover and simmer on low heat for 45 minutes. When cooked, remove and serve with sauce. Serves 6.

BROCCOLI AL MORO

I first tasted this dish at Al Moro in Rome some 15 years ago. It is a simple dish but a delightful way to cook broccoli.

¼ cup olive oil
1 tsp. minced garlic
4 cups fresh broccoli flowerets
1 cup Champagne
Salt & Pepper to your taste

Heat the oil in a heavy pan until very hot. Take off the heat and add the garlic. Return the pan to medium heat and add broccoli and toss until well coated. Add remaining ingredients and cook uncovered for five minutes. Cover and simmer for 15 minutes or until the broccoli is tender. Remove broccoli with slotted spoon to a hot platter, and reduce liquid to ½ cup. Pour over broccoli. Serves 4.

ANOTHER CALIFORNIA FIRST

The first California Champagne was produced in 1855 by Benjamin Davis Wilson in his San Gabriel winery. An adventurous Tennesseean, Wilson was a trapper, Indian trader, rancher, merchant, wine grower, state Senator and founder of Wilmington College, near Los Angeles.

Wilson never disclosed his method of making Champagne, which is a shame, because he obviously had an excellent product. Here are two newspaper accounts which praised his Champagne.

The *Los Angeles Star* in March 1855 quotes the *Alta California* published in San Francisco as follows: *"Mr. Wilson's experiment of making first quality Champagne wine promises to be entirely successful."*

One month later, the same newspaper quotes the *San Francisco Golden Era* as saying: *"B.D. Wilson, Esq. at his vineyard near the Mission of San Gabriel, is now engaged in the manufacture of a sparkling wine, which, as we have heard, promises to equal the best Champagne....."*

RED ONIONS BAKED IN CHAMPAGNE

Carol Huntsinger, wife of Korbel's Champagne maker, Jim Huntsinger, has a special recipe for red onions that are baked in Champagne. And she adds, you can serve these onions with anything from meat loaf to roast duckling.

2 medium sized red onions,
  peeled
2 tsp. melted butter
Salt & Pepper to your taste
8 Tbsp. Korbel Champagne

Cut the onions in half horizontally. Brush the cut sides with the melted butter. Then salt and pepper them. Set the onions in a shallow baking pan and bake, uncovered, for 30 minutes at 350 degrees. Remove the baking pan from the oven and pour 2 tablespoons of Champagne over each half. Return to the oven and bake another 30 minutes. Serves 2.

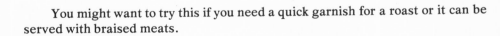

CHAMPAGNE BRAISED ONIONS

You might want to try this if you need a quick garnish for a roast or it can be served with braised meats.

18 small white onions, peeled
6 Tbsp. butter
2 tsp. sugar
¼ cup Champagne
Salt to taste

In a saucepan sear the onions until they are golden brown all over. Sprinkle in the sugar and shake the pan back and forth so the onions can brown and caramelize. Add the Champagne, cover and cook until the onions are done, about 20 minutes. Season with salt. Serves 4.

POTATOES IN CHAMPAGNE

Some people think the potato just might be the most important vegetable in the world. It wasn't always that way. Potatoes were once thought to cause leprosy, have been associated with wars and famine and the Scottish Presbyterians refused to eat them because they were not mentioned in the Bible.

Americans have been eating potatoes since 1719, thanks to the Irish immigrants who settled in New Hampshire. And we'll settle for the lovely potato to be married to the high and mighty wine, Champagne.

4 slices of bacon, diced in
*   1 inch pieces*
2 medium sized onions, thinly
*   sliced*
1 lb. potatoes, sliced ¼ inch
*   thick*
1 bay leaf
Salt and pepper to your taste
Brut Champagne

In a medium saucepan, sauté the bacon and onions over medium heat until the onions are soft. Add potatoes, bay leaf, salt and pepper. Pour enough Champagne in the pan to cover. Reduce the heat to simmer and cook 25 minutes covered or until the potatoes are done. Pour off sauce, reduce ⅓. Transfer potato mixture to heated serving platter and pour the sauce over them. Serves 4.

SAUERKRAUT COLMAR

This is an interesting dish. It has only four ingredients, and one of them is a whole bottle of Champagne.

4 slices of bacon, cut into
*   1 inch pieces*
1 lb. sauerkraut, well washed
1 cup diced dried apricots
1 bottle of dry Champagne

Combine all ingredients in a large saucepan. Cover and cook 1½ hours, stirring every 30 minutes. Serves 6.

ON DRINKING CHAMPAGNE

Champagne is created to be consumed immediately. You can store Champagne in your wine cellar, but it improves very little, if it improves at all.

Most Champagne producers, no matter what country of origin, will tell you that their product is ready to drink as soon as it is bottled.

CELERY STICKS

Most people serve celery mainly as an appetizer. They are usually stuffed with some kind of cheese or used with a dip. It is also used in soups, stuffings and stews. But very seldom is it served as a vegetable with the main course.

Here is a dish that is excellent with beef or ham. The secret is the slender celery "sticks" and the sauce.

> *2 cups celery, de-stringed, cut*
> *   into matchlike sticks about*
> *   2 inches long*
> *1 cup chicken stock*
> *1 tsp. dried tarragon*
> *3 whole cloves*
> *Champagne*
> *1 Tbsp. butter*
> *½ Tbsp. cornstarch*
> *Salt & Black pepper to your taste*

In a sauce pan combine the celery and chicken stock. Put the tarragon and cloves in a cheesecloth bag, tie it, and add to the pan. Cook until the celery is barely tender. Drain. Reserve cooking liquid. Discard bag. Add enough Champagne to the pan to make one cup of liquid. Blend butter and cornstarch until thoroughly mixed. Add to the liquid, stir until sauce is thick and smooth. Add salt and pepper. Add celery sticks, reheat quickly. Serves 6.

SAUTÉED CUCUMBERS

San Francisco model and socialite, Ursala Marsten, prefers Champagne to all other cocktails or wines and routinely greets her guests with an offer of a glass of Champagne. She is living testament to Madame Pompadour's statement that "Champagne is the only wine a woman can drink and remain beautiful. Ursala brings us this rare recipe from her native Germany and routinely serves it to her old friends, Alice Faye and Phil Harris.

> *7-8 large cucumbers, (Taste to*
> *   make sure they are not bitter)*
> *¼ lb. butter*
> *2 cups Dry Champagne*
> *Salt & white pepper to taste*
> *Fresh or dry Dill*

Peel cucumbers and dice into ½ inch cubes. Add to sauté pan with melted butter and Champagne. Simmer at medium heat until cucumbers become pale yellow in color, (about 20 to 25 minutes), stir occasionally. Serve with pan sauce which may be thickened with a little corn starch if you wish. Sprinkle the chopped dill on top. This dish is best served with steaks or red meat along with a second, more colorful vegetable. Serves 6.

CAULIFLOWER IN CHAMPAGNE SAUCE

Mark Twain once called cauliflower "cabbage with a college education." Maybe he was right for certainly cauliflower is one of the better vegetables that you can serve. While Americans like the creamy colored variety, there is a purple and green variety, usually seen only in Europe, especially Italy.

> *2½ lb. cauliflower, trimmed,*
>   *separated into flowerets*
> *¼ cup minced onions*
> *2 garlic cloves, minced*
> *⅓ cup olive oil*
> *½ tsp. thyme*
> *Salt & Pepper to your taste*
> *1½ cups dry Champagne*

Blanch the flowerets in boiling salt water for 3 minutes. Drain. Refresh in cold water and drain again. In a large saucepan, cook the garlic and onions in the oil until the onions are soft. Add flowerets, thyme, salt and pepper and sauté over high heat for 3 minutes. Add Champagne, bring to the boil, simmer for 8-10 minutes. With a slotted spoon transfer cauliflower to a warm platter. Reduce liquid to half and pour sauce over flowerets. Serves 6.

CHAMPAGNE GLAZED CARROTS

Carrots are known as the "mystery" food. No one seems to know when or where cultivated carrots developed. According to Joe Carcione in his delightful little book, *The Greengrocer*, he writes that carrots are still grown in Egypt with small purple roots while in Japan some giants are in excess of three feet.

Since fresh carrots are almost available the year around, you should be able to serve carrots cooked in Champagne the year around.

> *1½ lb. carrots, scraped and*
>   *quartered lengthwise and cut*
>   *into 2 inch lengths*
> *1 cup beef stock*
> *½ cup Champagne*
> *Salt and pepper to your taste*
> *6 Tbsp. butter*
> *2 Tbsp. chopped parsley*

Combine all the ingredients, except the parsley, into a saucepan. Cover, bring to the boil and then simmer for 25 to 30 minutes, or until the carrots are tender. When done, the liquid will have turned into a syrup sauce. Excess liquid can be eliminated by simmering the carrots uncovered. Before serving, sprinkle carrots with the parsley. Serves 6.

CAROTTES A LA CHAMPAGNE

And now we can mix carrots and onions with a little Champagne.

*24 pieces of carrots, trimmed and
    shaped like jumbo olives
24 small white onions
2 cups water
2 cups Champagne
6 Tbsp. butter
1 clove garlic, unpeeled*

Combine all ingredients in a large saucepan, cover and simmer 40 minutes. Remove the cover and simmer until the liquid becomes candied. Serves 4.

The victims of the San Francisco earthquake, as shaken as they were, received from a Moët et Chandon salesman in America a train car full of their house Champagne. That should have eased the shock of everything.

ZUCCHINI TRASTEVERE

I first tasted this dish late one afternoon in Rome. The Romans take at least two hours for lunch and my friend Nello was in no hurry to return to work. We had dined a little later than the noon hour at a small trattorie tucked away in the Trastevere section of Rome, one of the most secretive of places. The Frascati was cool, the bread sticks were crisp and the "pollo toscano alla diavolo" (chicken cooked in the style of Tuscany) was exceptional. With the chicken the chef served zucchini that was crisp, cooked with the onion, tomato and the famed Italian sparkling wine, Asti Spumante.

If you have ever tasted Asti Spumante, you know that it is slightly sweet. That's the way the Italians like it. The sweetness of the wine adds to the sautéed zucchini and you should try it before you turn your nose up.

*1 medium onion, chopped fine
1 Tbsp. butter
2 medium tomatoes, peeled,
    seeded and chopped
¼ cup Asti Spumante
1 lb. zucchini, cut into ½ inch
    rounds
¼ tsp. oregano
Salt & Pepper to your taste*

Cook the onion in the butter until the onion is just soft. Add tomatoes and wine. Cook until juice of tomatoes and wine are reduced by almost half. Add zucchini, oregano and salt and pepper. Cook until the zucchini is "al dente" or slightly crisp to the taste. Serves 6.

IX

Desserts

Probably there is not another part of a meal that is more pleasing to one's palate than dessert. Desserts play an important role in menu planning, because by the time one gets to dessert, the hunger pains have vanished.

Always try and serve a light dessert after a heavy meal and vice-versa. You wouldn't serve crepes as the main course and then offer a cake for dessert. You would be better to serve fresh fruit with a sweet Champagne.

Historically, Americans love desserts. It wasn't uncommon for farm hands to eat apple pie for breakfast while some fruit dessert was being prepared for supper that night.

Desserts are so highly favored in India that they are often served at the beginning of a meal, while in Greece sweet desserts are eaten anytime throughout the day. On the other hand, the Italians seldom eat pastries, preferring fresh fruit or cheese and this is the reason so many Italian restaurants have dessert specialities.

Champagne is such a great dessert by itself that some people prefer it alone. Others, like Leon Adams, author of *The Wines of America*, and internationally known as an authority on wines and spirits likes Champagne with strawberries. In his delightful book, *The Commonsense Book of Wine*, Mr. Adams writes "Sugar strawberries lightly and chill. Add pink Champagne for extra glamour and for a delicious dessert."

CRIBARI CHAMPAGNE JELLY

Champagne has an affinity for many fruits. Albert B. Cribari, vice president and winemaker at B. Cribari & Sons, shares with us his old family "Champagne Jelly" dessert recipe.

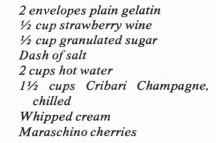

2 envelopes plain gelatin
½ cup strawberry wine
½ cup granulated sugar
Dash of salt
2 cups hot water
1½ cups Cribari Champagne,
*   chilled*
Whipped cream
Maraschino cherries

Soften gelatin in the strawberry wine. Add sugar, salt and hot water. Stir until sugar and gelatin dissolve. Chill until mixture begins to thicken. Whip Champagne quickly into slightly thickened gelatin. Pour into parfait glasses. Chill until firm. Top with whipped cream and cherries. Serves 6.

CHAMPAGNE SHERBET

Marilouise Kornell, the wife of Hanns Kornell, of Hanns Kornell Champagne Cellars in St. Helena, California, has many recipes that use Champagne as one of the ingredients. Here is her favorite.

2 cups water
1 cup sugar
1 cup orange juice
¼ cup lemon juice
2 cups Hanns Kornell Cham-
*   pagne, plus 6 Tbsp.*

Boil the water and sugar for 5 minutes. Add the orange and lemon juice. Cool. Stir in the Champagne and freeze. Divide the sherbet into six sherbet glasses and top with one tablespoon of Champagne. Serves 6.

SORBET ANANAS et CHAMPAGNE

They go by various names— ices, sorbets, sherbets and granitas. They were once exceptionally popular because they refreshed the palate between several long courses.

Not too long ago, the brilliant young French chef at Ernie's in San Francisco, Jacky Robert, changed the restaurant's menu and re-introduced what he calls sorbets. Here is one he created for the 14th annual Christian Brothers luncheon, which is always held at Ernie's.

1 ripe pineapple
¼ lb. sugar
½ bottle of Champagne

Cut the top of the pineapple one inch below the leaves. Empty the pineapple of its fruit with a spoon being very careful not to break the pineapple skin. Put the leaves and skin in the freezer. Put the fruit in a food processor for 15 seconds. Strain it. Add sugar and Champagne. Put the mixture in an ice cream freezer for 20 minutes. Place the sorbet into the pineapple shell and keep it in the food freezer until ready to serve. Serves 6.

FRUITS IN CHAMPAGNE

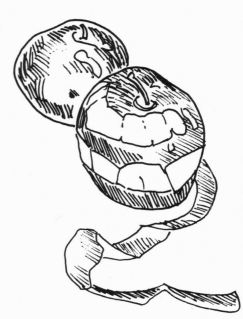

Here is another one of those simple easy desserts that take so little time to prepare, and is so good to eat.

1 apple, cut into bite size pieces
1 pear, cut into bite size pieces
1 orange, peeled and cut into bite
   size pieces
1 grapefruit, peeled and cut into
   bite size pieces
½ cup seedless grapes
Champagne

Combine all fruits in a bowl, mix well and chill for two hours. Just before serving, pour the Champagne over the fruit. Serves 4.

CHAMPAGNE BAKED ALASKA

The following recipe for Champagne Baked Alaska was submitted by Ken Hoop of the Wine Appreciation Guild.

> *4 one-half-inch thick slices of pound cake*
> *12 Tbsp. Champagne (Demi-Sec*
>   *or Spumante)*
> *1 quart Vanilla with raspberry*
>   *swirl ice cream*
> *6 egg whites*
> *1⅛ cup sugar*
> *¾ tsp. salt*
> *¼ tsp. vanilla extract*
> *Ruby Port*
> *Powdered Sugar*

Pre-heat oven to 475 degrees. Trim corners off slices of cake to conform to rounded scoop of ice cream. Arrange slices of cake on platter and pour 3 tablespoons of champagne or spumante over each. Set aside and allow cake to absorb wine. In large mixing bowl beat egg whites with electric beater. When they have risen well, gradually add salt, sugar and vanilla extract and continue beating until a stiff meringue has formed. Put into pastry tube to decorate. With spatula arrange soaked slices of cake spaciously on large cookie sheet. Top each cake slice with one scoop of solidly frozen ice cream. Drizzle Ruby Port over each scoop of ice cream. With pastry tube start where cake meets ice cream and go around and around ice cream until totally covered by ½ to ¾ inch layer of meringue. IMPORTANT: NO ICE CREAM SHOULD BE EXPOSED TO AIR. Finished shape will be a rounded pyramid. Slide into pre-heated HOT oven and bake for 3 to 4 minutes until edges of meringue are golden. Remove from oven and sprinkle with powdered sugar. With spatula place onto dessert dishes and serve immediately. Some of the same sweet champagne will accompany this course nicely. Serves 4.

MOUSSE au CHAMPAGNE de LAURENT PERRIER

Hank Rubin has been writing the **WINEMASTER** column for the San Francisco Chronicle since 1965. Previous to that he was Executive Chef at the Pot Luck restaurant in Berkeley. During those years, Mr. Rubin would offer on the first Monday in April a special Anniversary dinner. It was at the third anniversary dinner that he offered as dessert, Mousse au Champagne de Laurent Perrier.

But before we get to the dessert, here's what Mr. Rubin offered you for the high figure of $5.50 (wines, tax and tip extra).

* Potage de Epinards a la Patricia (a spinach purée with eggs and cheese.)

* Salad de Orange et de Pamplemousse Vinaigrette (orange and grapefruit salad with black olives, onions, mint and parsley.)

* Crepes de Avocat Fracis Avec Crabe (crèpes made with avocado pulp and filled with Dungeness crab in a cream sauce.)

* Filet de Boeuf Gourmet, Sauce Béarnaise (brandy marinated filet, with sauce béarnaise.)

* Artichauts Farcis (artichoke hearts stuffed with mushrooms and ham.)

* Purée de Marrons aux Celeri (purée of chestnuts with finely diced celery.)

* Creme de Carottes (carrot cream with orange.)

In addition, there were 10 wines to choose from, like a 1949 Grand Echezeaux, 1949 Chateau Latour or the great 1959 Winkeler Hasensprung Trockenbeerenauslese.

And the dessert.

1 Tbsp. plain gelatin
¼ cup cold water
4 egg yolks
3 whole eggs
6 oz. granulated sugar
9 oz. Champagne
4 egg whites beaten stiffly
1 cup heavy cream, beaten stiffly
Candied violets (optional)

Soften the gelatin in the cold water. Beat together in the top of a double boiler the yolks and whole eggs. Add the sugar and Champagne. Place the mixture over hot water and cook, stirring steadily until thickened. Add softened gelatin and mix until dissolved. Cool. Fold in egg whites and heavy cream. Pour into individual serving dishes. Add candied violets. Serves 10 - 12.

GAMAY BEAUJOLAIS SHERBET

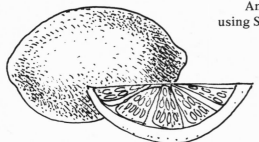

And over in San Jose, Norbert Mirassou has his own special sherbet recipe using Sparkling Gamay Beaujolais.

2 cups mini-marshmallows
1 cup boiling water
Grated rind of 1 lemon
1   bottle Mirassou Sparkling
*   Gamay Beaujolais*
Juice of 1 lemon
¼ cup Grenadine

Dissolve the marshmallows in the boiling water. Add lemon rind and cool to room temperature. Add remaining ingredients. Put in ice cream freezer and rotate until it becomes sherbet. If you use the freezer in your refrigerator, it will take about 4-6 hours. Serves 6.

GRANITE au CHAMPAGNE

Since Domaine Chandon has opened its sparkling wine cellars and restaurant in Yountville, thousands of people have flocked to take the tour and taste the food. Chef Philippe Jeanty has been very busy, but took some time off to pass along this recipe for his version of a refreshing between course palate pleaser.

1 bottle Domaine Chandon Napa
*   Valley Brut*
½ cup sugar (maximum - adjust
*   to personal taste)*
1 tsp. Kirsch

Mix all ingredients quickly, just enough to blend and dissolve the sugar.(CAUTION: Too much blending will cause most of the lightness to escape with the wine's bubbles.) Freeze the mixture in a shallow pan for two hours or longer until very firm. To serve, scrape the surface of the ice with a spoon to make a small ball of shavings. Serves 4 - 6.

PEACH CHAMPAGNE SOUP

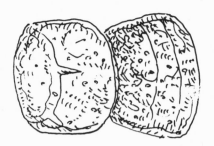

Ever serve soup for dessert? Don't laugh. In the Nordic countries, fruit soups as a dessert have been served there for several hundred years. Try this dessert at your next dinner party.

6 medium ripe peaches
1 quart scalding water
½ bottle white wine
Sugar to your taste
½ bottle Champagne

Put the peaches in a wire basket and dip them into the scalding water for one minute. Peel the skins off the peaches, cut them in half and remove the pits. Put the peaches in a deep bowl and cover with the white wine. Add sugar, cover and chill two hours. To serve, put one peach half in a dish, cover with 1/6th of the wine marinade and pour an equal amount of Champagne over it. Serves 6.

QUICK SUMMER DESSERT

Here is an exceptional quick summer dessert. Fill a tall parfait glass ¾ full with shaved ice. Make a hole in the shaved ice about ¼ inch in diameter. Pour Cherry Heering into the hole to fill. Now fill the glass with Champagne. Serves 1.

CHAMPAGNE APPLES

One of the better ways of ending a meal is with fruit. One fruit that seems to be available almost the year around is apples.

1 Tbsp. dried muscat raisins
¼ cup Champagne
1 medium apple, cored & halved
1 tsp. sugar
½ tsp. fresh grated lime/lemon
  peel
¼ tsp. cinnamon
1 tsp. butter

Drop the muscat raisins into the Champagne for 30 minutes. This will plump them. In a small baking dish, place the apple halves face up. Drain the raisins and reserve the wine. Mix raisins with sugar, lime/lemon peel and cinnamon. Divide this mixture in two and top the apples with it. Divide the butter in half and top the apples. Pour over the reserved wine. Bake 25-30 minutes in a 350 degree oven. Spoon juices over apples when serving. Serves 2.

Cincinnati, Ohio is the birth-place of American Champagne. In the spring of 1847, Nicholas Longworth successfully produced the first bottle of Champagne in America. The good news spread because by 1855 California was producing sparkling wine, and New York State by 1863.

Longworth experiences, as told by Paul Fredericksen of the Wine Institute in *Wine Review*, June and July issues of 1947, are as follows:

Longworth found as others had that grape vines from Europe would not flourish in the Eastern States, so he turned to native varieties. He was particularly attracted to the Catawba. Longworth used the Catawba in his winery year after year.

One day in 1842 he reached into his bin and brought out a bottle for sampling. He drew the cork and poured some of the wine into a glass. To his surprise, it seethed and sparkled with tiny carbonic acid gas bubbles that had developed and become imprisoned in it.

That was 133 years ago.

SPUMANTE FLOAT

Many times the simplest of ingredients combined in the correct proportion, will give us the best results. Rosemary Papagni-Vallis of Papagni Vineyards passes along this excellent dessert.

> *6 tall float glasses*
> *½ gallon French vanilla ice cream*
> *2 cups fresh raspberries*
> *1 bottle of Angelo Papagni "Spumante d'Angelo"*

Alternate layers of ice cream and raspberries in the float glasses until they are ¾ full. Fill the remaining ¼ with Spumante d'Angelo. Serves 6.

CHAMPAGNE KIR SORBET

And according to Mildred Howie, who handles the public relations activities of Korbel Champagne, here is a fine sorbet, often served by Gary and Marilou Heck.

> *3 cups Korbel Brut Champagne*
> *½ cup sugar*
> *1 tsp. creme de cassis*

Mix the above in a large bowl and stir until the sugar is dissolved. Pour into a freezing tray and freeze for about five hours. Remove to a chilled bowl and beat with electric beater until smooth. Return it to the freezer for three to six hours. Serve in chilled wine glasses. Serves 6.

MARQUISE AU CHAMPAGNE

Fruit for dessert is fast becoming a must for everyone. And when a bottle of Champagne is introduced into the scene, it makes this dessert all the better to taste.

½ lb. raspberries
½ lb. strawberries
1 cup granulated sugar
Juice of 1 lemon
1 bottle dry Champagne

Wash the fruit and discard any that are not suitable for eating. Put them in a medium sized glass bowl. Add remaining ingredients and let macerate for an hour. Divide the mixture in six and put into tall Champagne glasses. Serves 6.

The next time you open a bottle of Champagne and would like to make a toast other than "Cheers", we would like to suggest:

ZULA.....Oogy Wawa
GREECE.....Ygeia
DENMARK.....Skoal
ESPERANTO.....Je zia sano
SPAIN.....Salud
RUSSIA.....Vashe Zdorovie
FRANCE.....Santé
GERMANY.....Prosit
JAPAN.....Kampai
CHINA.....Yum Shing
HAWAII.....Okolole Maluna
ITALY.....Cincin
ISRAEL.....Lechaim
IRELAND.....Slainte
For me personally.....Ahhhhhh

WATERMELON WITH CHAMPAGNE

Mary Lester, the syndicated columnist and author of *Hand Me That Corkscrew, Bacchus*, shares Oliver Goulet's special way with watermelon.

1 large ripe watermelon
Pink Champagne to fill

Make a large plug in the melon. Fill with Pink Champagne and chill for three hours. Serve in slices. For a different taste treat, poke some holes in the melon, insert straws and sip away.

COUPE DE LUXE

The Taylor Wine Company, Inc. has been making wines since 1880 and Champagne since 1941. From their kitchens comes this recipe for a fruit dessert.

1 pint fresh strawberries or
whole frozen
1-10 oz. package frozen sliced
peaches, defrosted with juice
1-15 oz. can pineapple chunks,
drained
½ cup brandy
1 bottle Taylor New York State
Extra Dry Champagne

Combine fruits and brandy in a bowl, refrigerate one hour. Spoon into 6 individual serving glasses. Pour Champagne over the fruit. Serves 6.

MARSHALL'S MELON BALLS IN CHAMPAGNE

My friend Jim Marshall is an extraordinary cook. He has a marvelous touch with sauces and his attention to vegetables is worthy of a class in technique alone. Here is his excellent, but simple recipe for a special dessert.

24 melon or canteloupe balls
1 bottle of Champagne

Put six melon balls into a fluted Champagne glass. Pour Champagne to fill. Repeat five more times. Serves 6.

CHAMPAGNE SABAYON WITH BLACKBERRIES

Blackberries are native to Asia, Europe and North America. They are members of the rose family and that's why when you find them wild or grow them in your backyard, you have to be careful of the thorns when you pick them at harvest time.

> *1 pint blackberries*
> *6 egg yolks**
> *1 cup sugar*
> *½ bottle of brut Champagne*

Divide the blackberries into 6 portions. In the top of your double boiler, beat the yolks and sugar until lemon colored. Gradually add Champagne. Place the mixture over hot water and cook, slowly, always stirring, until the mixture is thick and creamy. Pour over blackberries which have been put into large parfait glasses. Serves 6.

*NOTE— The 6 egg whites can be frozen and used for soufflés.

Lord Chesterfield's favorite toast was:
> *"Give me Champagne and fill it to the brim*
> *I'll toast in bumpers every lovely limb."*

CHAMPAGNE MIST

Here is an excellent dessert when the strawberry season is in full bloom.

> *1 cup fresh strawberries,*
> *chopped in half*
> *2 Tbsp. Irish Mist liqueur*
> *1 pint vanilla ice cream*
> *Champagne, chilled*

Mix strawberries and liqueur, cover and chill for 1 hour. Divide the ice cream equally and out into 4 large wine glasses. Spoon strawberry mixture equally among the 4 glasses. Fill the glasses with Champagne. Serves 4.

CHAMPAGNE ZABAGLIONE

This is a marriage of Italian and French ingredients. The recipe is from *Feasts of a Militant Gastronome* written by Robert Courtine, who is by all odds one of the most influential food writers in France.

6 egg yolks
⅔ cup sugar
1 cup Champagne (Pol Roger,
*   says Mr. Courtine)*
1 vanilla bean
Grated rind of 1 lemon

Whisk the yolks and sugar together until mixed. Slowly add the Champagne. Then add vanilla bean and lemon rind. Place the mixture over hot water bath and whisk slowly until well mixed. Serve in Champagne glasses. Serves 4.

ORANGES IN CHAMPAGNE

The great gourmet Andre L. Simon, who founded the Wine and Food Society said that *"Champagne has always been, still is, and will ever be an extravagant wine and the most charming and fascinating of wines."*

3 oranges, peeled and sliced
½ cup sugar
¼ cup Armagnac
Champagne

Put the sliced oranges in a bowl and top with sugar. Add Armagnac and chill for 4 hours. Spoon fruit and liquid into six serving dishes and add Champagne to taste. Serves 6.

X

Potpourri

potpourri (Fr.) A medley or miscellany; mixture.

That's the way Webster defines potpourri. We agree. And so here for your inspection is a potpourri, a mixture of recipes using Champagne, a medley of various things to tease the palate. There is something for everyone, a taste, a treat to stimulate the gustatory senses, to prickle your epicurean delights, to whisk you to new heights.

Leslie Charteris, creator of that modern Robin Hood, Simon Templar, better known as "The Saint", once wrote a column for Gourmet magazine. In it he displayed his love of good food and wine just as Simon Templar liked good food and wine.

Throughout the more than 40 volumes of Saintly adventures of Simon Templar, Charteris often uses food and wine as a means of showing the "gourmet" side of the Saint.

I became a devoted Saint fan back at Christmas 1940 when my Mother gave me my first Saint book, The Saint Goes On. I read it and from that moment on became addicted to all of the Saint's exploits.

What brought this all back to me was the announcement some time ago by my friend Bob McKendrick, publisher of the Sausalito Revue, that he was forming a "Society of Saints". It is an association for those who are Saint addicts as well as lovers of food and wine, something Bob calls a literary/gourmet association. The first meeting was extraordinary and the future is very bright for this organization. In fact, Simon Templar would be pleased to know that such fine people are following in his buccaneering ways.

"Breakfast with him," wrote Mr. Charteris about the Saint in the story, "The Unusual Ending," was always a sober meal, to be eaten with a proper respect for the gastronomic virtues of grilled bacon and whatever delicacy was mated with it. On this morning it was mushrooms, a dish that had it's own unapproachable place in the Saint's ideal of a day's beginning; and he had dealt with them slowly and lusciously, as they deserved, with golden wafers of brown toast on their port side and an open newspaper propped up against the coffee pot for scanning to the starboard."

SOUFFLÉ AU TEMPLAR

And it is with proper respect that we offer the following recipe for all those not so saintly modern Robin Hoods and our fellow "Saints of Society."

4 eggs separated
⅔ cup sugar
1 lime, grated rind & juice
3 Tbsp. sweet Champagne
1 extra egg white

Beat yolks until thick. Gradually add sugar, stirring. Mix rind, lime juice and Champagne. Beat whites plus extra white until stiff peaks form. Fold whites into yolk mixture. Butter and sugar a 4 cup soufflé mold. Pour mixture into soufflé mold and bake 25 minutes at 375 degrees. Serves 4.

CHAMPAGNE SAUCE

Our first presentation is a simple sauce, one that can be used for numerous desserts.

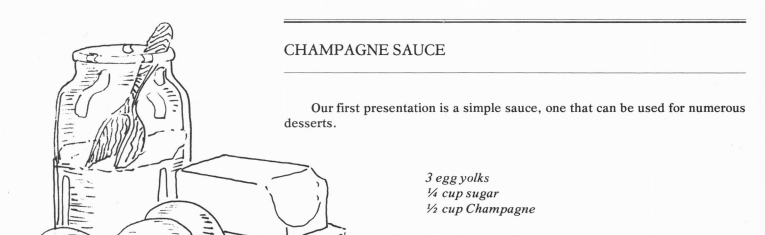

3 egg yolks
¼ cup sugar
½ cup Champagne

Combine the yolks and sugar in a double boiler set over simmering water. Beat the mixture with a wire whisk until it becomes thick and lemon colored. Add the Champagne gradually. Continue to beat the mixture until it is light and foamy. Makes 2 cups.

CHAMPAGNE STEAK SAUCE

Now we offer a fine Champagne sauce for your best grilled steaks.

1 Tbsp. shallots, minced
2 Tbsp. butter
1 Tbsp. Dijon style mustard
2 tsp. parsley, minced
1 cup brut Champagne
Salt and Pepper to your taste

In a sauté pan, cook the shallots in the butter until soft. Add mustard, parsley, Champagne and salt and pepper. Cook over the simmer until the sauce is reduced by half. Pour over steaks as they come off the grill. Serves 2 - 4.

Do you have a favorite Bearnaise Sauce recipe? If so, that recipe must call for the use of a white wine. Our suggestion is to substitute Champagne for the white wine. Try it. You'll like it.

CHAMPAGNE & CHIVE SAUCE

You've got just barely an hour to fix dinner. There's a chicken in the refrigerator, carrots and green beans. You can quickly sauté the chicken and prepare the vegetables, but you haven't got several hours to make a sauce for the chicken. If you've ever had that problem, here is your answer.

½ cup Champagne
1 Tbsp. chopped chives
1 Tbsp. butter
1 Tbsp. flour
Salt and Pepper to your taste
6 grinds fresh nutmeg

Put the Champagne into a small sauce pan and boil it for 5 minutes. Add the chopped chives. Mix the butter and flour together and add it to the pan along with the remaining ingredients. Cook slowly until the mixture thickens. Makes enough sauce for a medium sized chicken.

CHAMPAGNE DRESSING—1

As we turn to eating more and more vegetables, we need better and better salad dressings. For your dining pleasure, here are two Champagne salad dressings, one a little more complicated than the other, but both excellent. The first dressing is made right at the table, which will impress your guests. The second dressing is bottled and left to marry before using.

½ cup olive oil
1 Tbsp. lemon juice
Salt & Pepper to your taste
½ cup iced Champagne

In a medium sized bowl, combine the first three ingredients and mix well with a wire whisk. When well blended, pour in the Champagne, stirring just enough to blend the Champagne with the other ingredients. Serves 2.

CHAMPAGNE DRESSING— 2

2 cups olive oil
¼ cup Champagne
½ cup red wine vinegar
Salt & Pepper to your taste
½ tsp. dry mustard
½ tsp. dried basil
½ tsp. dried oregano
1 clove garlic, peeled

Put all ingredients into a food processor or blender and mix until creamy. Pour into a bottle and let stand a few hours, or a few days before serving. Makes 3 cups.

CHAMPAGNE DRESSING

Many years ago, on my first trip to France, I stayed at the Hotel Edouard VII on the Avenue de la Opera in Paris. Next to the hotel was a restaurant called Delmonico. It was here that I first tasted an 1888 Armagnac, a sea bass stuffed with shrimp and coated with Béarnaise sauce and a Champagne dressing tossed with my salad.

For months after that trip I tried to duplicate the dressing recipe. I must have tried a hundred combinations, all without success. I abandoned the project, only to return a month later and on the first try succeed.

> *6 Tbsp. French walnut oil**
> *¼ cup dry Champagne*
> *Salt & White pepper to your taste*

Put all the ingredients into a glass bowl. Whip briskly until the mixture is smooth and foamy. Serves 3. *NOTE: If you can't get walnut oil, get French olive oil. It is lighter than other olive oils.

CHAMPAGNE MAYONNAISE

Here is a mayonnaise using Champagne. I've included this recipe because there are so many variations of the original Mayonnaise recipe. Champagne used in this recipe is to thin out the mixture, and does play an overall part in the final taste. NOTE: Please have all the ingredients in this recipe at room temperature.

> *2 egg yolks*
> *1 tsp. of salt*
> *½ tsp. dry mustard*
> *1 pint of the best grade olive oil*
> *Champagne*

In a shallow bowl, use a wire whisk to beat the yolks, salt and mustard together. Now add the oil, a few drops at a time, always beating the mixture with the whisk. Keep up this slow process until the mixture is thick and somewhat stiff. Now thin it with the Champagne to reach the desired consistency. Makes 2 cups.

One of the oldest proverbs in Champagne is:

"Who buys good wine will taste and drink good wine."

CHINESE CHAMPAGNE BARBECUE SAUCE

Outdoor grilling is so popular today that some manufacturers have a tough time coming up with new ideas. But chefs are always coming up with new creations.

1 cup soy sauce
½ cup Champagne
3 Tbsp. red wine
1 Tbsp. sugar
1 tsp. salt
1 clove garlic, peeled & crushed

Combine all ingredients. Mix well with wire whisk. Let stand at least one hour. Use to baste broiled spareribs. Makes 1½ cups.

FONDUE AU CHAMPAGNE

For informal parties, there is nothing better than a fondue. And when you add as well as serve Champagne, it becomes an affair to remember.

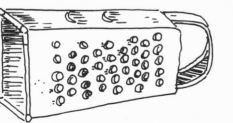

1 Tbsp. flour
2 cups grated Gruyère cheese
2 cups grated Emmenthal cheese
1 cup of Champagne
2 Tbsp. brandy
Fresh ground black pepper
Cubes of French bread

Toss the cheese in the flour. Place the cheese in a heavy pan along with the Champagne. Add brandy and black pepper and stir for five minutes. Keep the fondue warm over a table burner. Serve bread cubes with long fondue forks for dipping. Serves 4.

CHAMPAGNE MARINATED AVOCADO SALAD

San Francisco socialite, Ursala Marsten, has developed this exotic and easy way to serve avocados. It is ideal for a summer buffet or picnic and was a real favorite of band leader, Harry James.

⅓ cup salad oil
½ cup white wine vinegar
3 cups dry Champagne
2 tsp. sugar
2 tsp. salt
Ground pepper to your taste
6-8 ripe avocados
1 box cherry tomatoes
2-3 medium sized onions
1 head butter lettuce
Parsley to garnish

Put the first six ingredients into a bottle and allow them to stand while preparing the salad. Peel avocados and slice lengthwise into ½ inch slices, place in salad bowl along with cherry tomatoes cut in half. Alternate layers with thin slices of onion. Shake marinade, pour over salad and let stand in refrigerator for 4 to 6 hours. Serve on lettuce leaves and garnish with chopped parsley. Serves 6.

By 1739, Champagne had become so popular in Paris, the city gave a brilliant ball in which some 1,800 bottles of Champagne were consumed. Only 500 people attended.

MARILOUISE KORNELL'S HOT SAUCE

If you need a quick hot Champagne sauce for those hot or cold puddings, or just a topping for some fruit, Marilouise Kornell has just the answer.

1½ cups Kornell Champagne
* Rouge*
½ cup sugar
Grated rind of ½ lemon
2 crushed cloves
1 one-inch piece of cinnamon stick

Combine all the ingredients in an enameled saucepan and simmer for five minutes. Strain through a fine seive or cheesecloth.

Lastly, experiment with Champagne. Substitute it when necessary. Create your own dishes. Change. Modify. Never stop. This is the essence of devising new dishes, new tastes and new techniques.

And . . . . . .always, ALWAYS pause for a glass of Champagne.

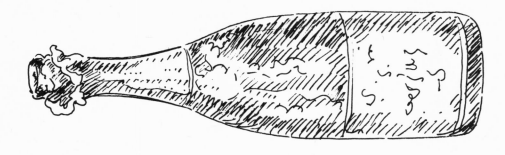

"One's Brut is another's Sec" — Malcolm R. Hébert

Index

The Wine Advisory Board Cookbooks
"The Classic Series on Cooking With Wine"

This series of seven wine cookbooks is the largest collection of cooking with wine recipes available in the World. There is no duplication of features or recipes in the Wine Advisory Board Cookbooks. Specific wine types are recommended as table beverages for all main dishes. The present series represents over 2,900 different recipes of all types using wine. From wine cocktails, hors d'oeuvres, salads, soups, wild game, fish, eggs, many different main dishes to desserts and jellies; the magnitude of this collection of wine recipes is overwhelming. Who could possibly develop and test such a large number of recipes? These books are the result of the cooperation of over 400 people in the wine industry. In 1961 the Wine Advisory Board began collecting the favorite and best recipes of the various winemakers and their families. Most of the recipes are old family favorites, tested with time and then re-tested and proven in Wine Advisory Board test kitchens. We are particularly pleased with the recipes and wine choices from staff members of the Department of Viticulture and Enology and the Department of Food Science and Technology of University of California, Davis and Fresno.

So here is a series of the very best wine recipes; selected and developed by many of the most knowledgeable wine and food lovers of America.

#500 EPICUREAN RECIPES OF CALIFORNIA WINEMAKERS: Did you know that you can buy wild boar, cook it at home with Burgundy and produce a gourmet treat that your guests will rave about for years? Or, that you can make your reputation as an Epicurean cook by preparing and serving Boeuf ala Bourguignonne, according to the recipe of a famous wine authority? This book includes the most elaborate to simple recipes contributed by California Winemakers, their wives and associates; all selected for their unforgettable taste experiences. Another important feature of this book is the comprehensive index of recipes for the entire six cookbook series. 128 pp, 8½"x11", illustrated, 1978 edition. $5.95 @ ISBN 0-932664-00-8

#501 GOURMET WINE COOKING THE EASY WAY: All new recipes for memorable eating, prepared quickly and simply with wine. Most of the recipes specify convenience foods which can be delightfully flavored with wine, enabling the busy homemaker to set a gourmet table for family and friends with a minimum of time in the kitchen. More than 500 tested and proven recipes; used frequently by the first families of America's wine industry. 128pp, 8½"x11", illustrated, 1980 edition. $5.95 @ ISBN 0-932664-01-6

#502 ADVENTURES IN WINE COOKERY BY CALIFORNIA WINEMAKERS: New Revised 1980 Edition, Includes many new Recipes from California's new winemakers. The life work of the winemaker is to guide nature in the development in wine of beauty, aroma, bouquet and subtle flavors. Wine is part of their daily diet, leading to more flavorful dishes, comfortable living, merriment and goodfellowship. These recipes contributed by Winemakers, their families and colleagues represent this spirit of flavorful good living. A best selling cookbook with 500 exciting recipes including barbecue, wine drinks, salads and sauces. 128pp, illustrated, 8½"x11", $5.95 @ ISBN 0-932664-10-5

#503 FAVORITE RECIPES OF CALIFORNIA WINEMAKERS: The original winemakers' cookbook and a bestseller for fifteen years. Over 200 dedicated winemakers, their wives and colleagues have shared with us their love of cooking. They are the authors of this book, which is dedicated to a simple truth known for thousands of years in countless countries: good food is even better with wine. Over 500 authentic recipes, many used for generations, are included in this "cookbook classic". 128pp, 8½"x11", illustrated, $4.95 @ ISBN 0-932664-03-2

#504 WINE COOKBOOK OF DINNER MENUS by Emily Chase and Wine Advisory Board. Over 100 complete dinner menus with recommended complimentary wines. This book will make your dinner planning easy and the results impressive to your family and most sophisticated guests. Emily Chase worked with the winemakers of California a number of years and was also the Home Economics Editor of Sunset Magazine. She tested recipes for six years and is the author of numerous articles and books on cooking. This edition contains 400 different recipes, suggestions for wines to accompany dinners and tips on serving, storing and enjoying wine. 128pp, illustrated, 8½"x11", 1978 edition $4.95 @ ISBN 0-932664-04-0

#505 EASY RECIPES OF CALIFORNIA WINEMAKERS: "I wonder often what vintners buy one-half so precious as the stuff they sell" questioned Omar Khayyam 1100 A.D. We wonder what the vintners could possibly eat one-half so delicious as the food they prepare. This is a collection of "precious" recipes that are easy to prepare and each includes the vintners favorite beverage. Many are recipes concocted in the vintners kitchens and some are family favorites proven for their flavor and ease of preparation. No duplication with the other cookbooks. 128pp, illustrated, 8½"x11", $4.95 @ ISBN 0-932664-05-9

#640 THE CHAMPAGNE COOKBOOK: "Add Some Sparkle to Your Cooking and Your Life" by Malcolm R. Hebert. Cooking with Champagne is a glamorous yet easy way to liven up your cuisine. The recipes range from soup, salads, hors d'oeuvres, fish, fowl, red meat, vegetables and of course desserts—all using Champagne. Many new entertaining ideas with Champagne cocktails, drinks and Champagne lore are included along with simple rules on cooking with and serving Sparkling Wines. Recipes are provided by California, New York and European Champagne makers and their families. The author's 30 years of teaching and writing about food and wine makes this an elegant yet practical book. 128pp, illustrated, 8½" x 11" ppb, $5.95 @ ISBN 0-932664-07-5

ADDITIONAL WINE BOOKS PUBLISHED BY THE WINE APPRECIATION GUILD

#641 THE POCKET ENCYCLOPEDIA OF CALIFORNIA WINE by William I. Kaufman. A convenient and thorough reference book that fits into your vest pocket and gives answers to all of your questions about California Wines. All the wineries, grape varieties, wines, geography and wine terms are covered briefly and authoritatively by one of America's foremost wine experts. Carry with you to restaurants and wine tastings to make you well informed on your choice of California Wines. 128 compact pages, 7¾" x 3½" with vinyl cover. $3.95 @ ISBN 0-932664-09-1, June 1980

#527 IN CELEBRATION OF WINE AND LIFE: "The fascinating Story of Wine and Civilization." by Richard Lamb & Ernest Mittelberger. With art reproductions from The Wine Museum of San Francisco. The origins, customs and traditions of winemaking and wine drinking explored in depth and explained through the art work and lore of wine through the ages. Such important subjects as wine and health and wine and love are covered as well as the hows and whys of selecting, cellaring and appreciating wine. 35 Full Color plates and many rare prints richly illustrate this intriguing book. Revised 1980 Edition, 248pp, quality paperback, 10" x 8", $9.95 @ ISBN 0-932664-13-X

#554 WINE CELLAR RECORD BOOK: A professionally planned, elegant, leatherette bound cellar book for the serious wine collector. Organized by the wine regions of the World, helpful for keeping perpetual inventories and monitoring the aging of each wine in your cellar. Enough space for over 200 cases of wine and space to record tasting notes and special events. Illustrated 12" x 10½", six ring binder, additional pages available. $29.95 @ ISBN 0-932664-06-7

Each book includes its own index; however, **EPICUREAN RECIPES** includes a comprehensive index for the entire cookbook series. These books are available at bookstores, wine shops and wineries. If you have trouble finding them, they may be ordered direct from The Wine Appreciation Guild. Also, most other wine books and wine related items are available.

HOW TO ORDER BY MAIL: Indicate the number of copies and titles you wish on the order form below and include your check, money order, or MasterCharge, or VISA card number. California residents include 6% sales tax. There is a $1.00 shipping and handling charge per order, regardless of how many books you order. (If no order form—any paper will do.) Orders shipped promptly via U.S. Mail—U.S. & Canada shipments ONLY.

ORDER FORM
WINE APPRECIATION GUILD
1377 Ninth Avenue
San Francisco, California 94122

SHIP TO: _____

Address _____ City _____ State _____ Zip _____

Please send the following:

_____ Copies, #500 EPICUREAN RECIPES OF CALIFORNIA WINEMAKERS,	$5.95@	_____
_____ Copies, #501 GOURMET WINE COOKING THE EASY WAY,	$5.95@	_____
_____ Copies, #502 ADVENTURES IN WINE COOKERY,	$5.95@	_____
_____ Copies, #503 FAVORITE RECIPES OF CALIFORNIA WINEMAKERS,	$4.95@	_____
_____ Copies, #504 WINE COOKBOOK OF DINNER MENUS,	$4.95@	_____
_____ Copies, #505 EASY RECIPES OF CALIFORNIA WINEMAKERS,	$4.95@	_____
_____ Copies, #640 THE CHAMPAGNE COOKBOOK,	$5.95@	_____
_____ Copies, #527 IN CELEBRATION OF WINE & LIFE,	$9.95@	_____
_____ Copies, #554 WINE CELLAR RECORD BOOK,	$29.95@	_____
_____ Copies, #641 POCKET ENCYCLOPEDIA OF CALIFORNIA WINES,	$3.95@	
	Subtotal	_____
California Residents 6% sales tax		_____
Plus $1.00 Shipping and handling (per order)		$1.00
TOTAL enclosed or charged to credit card		_____

Please charge to my Mastercharge   or VISA card   # _____

Expiration Date _____ Signature _____